Goodwill on Credit

Travels in Ireland

By Gerry Britt

© 2014 Gerry Britt

All rights reserved. This book or any portion thereof may not be reproduced or used in any manner whatsoever without the express written permission of the publisher except for the use of brief quotations in a book review, and certain other noncommercial uses permitted by copyright law.

Published by Goodwill on Credit Publications

First release: July 2014

ISBN-13: 978-0986210006

FORWARD

This is a collection of stories written over the course of several years covering numerous visits to Ireland. While it contains some (hopefully) useful travel and tourist tips, the collection is mostly concerned with the wonderful things that happen between points A and B on the tourist map, and the people (and the occasional animal) that inhabit those in-between places.

My most cherished memories of Ireland, and the things that I now return to, cannot be found on a map. I hope that this humble volume will inspire you to experience the places in between the destinations, for there you will find the true Ireland.

Hills as green as emeralds
Cover the countryside.
Lakes as blue as sapphires
Are Ireland's special pride.
And rivers that shine like silver
Make Ireland look so fair.
But the friendliness of her people
Is the richest treasure there.

ACKNOWLEDGEMENTS

Really, I'd like to thank everyone I've ever met in Ireland. I'll settle for thanking all the Britts and Holohans; the villages of Upperchurch and Drombane, aka Heaven on Earth; my constant friends and hosts the Morrows, Butlers, Kinnanes, and Condons; Kildare's best, Kenny "The American" Pitt. I love you all and I'll see you soon.

A special thank you to Maxmedia and their work with Tourism Ireland, for their generosity, guidance and expertise in all things Irish.

To my wife and son, thank you for indulging my dreams.

For My Brother

Contents

FORWARD i
ACKNOWLEDGEMENTS ii
Dublin All the Time 1
How to Pack for Ireland in Two Easy Steps 9
Once Upon a Time in Belfast 14
Why in the World Would He Leave? 21
Get Me to the Islands, Seanie 25
The Boys of Ballyfinnane 31
The Hounds of Bandon (And Other Irish Beasts) 40
Urlingford 46
The Euro Considered, or, I'm Putting a Hotel on Marvin Gardens 60
Derry, or The Slash, or Together in All But Name 68
Ah, the People… 78
Irish Poker 89
Mind Yourself, Now 102
Avoiding the PITS*: A Handy Guide to Beating the Blues after the Green (*Post-Ireland Travel Syndrome) 106
About the Author 112

Dublin All the Time

If you're expecting a tourist's paean to this fair city, skip this part. Dublin *is* a great place to spend a day, a weekend, or a week, but I've spent enough time there to be able to look past the wonderful heart of the city and focus on the lifeblood that flows along its avenues. Not literally, of course—that doesn't happen anymore, even in Belfast. What follows are my observations while doing nothing more than watching the world go by. Non-smoking hotel rooms provide excellent opportunities for this by forcing you outside.

~

I sipped coffee from a paper cup and smoked on the steps of O'Callaghan's Hotel across from Merrion Square and watched the world go by. Dublin on a weekday morning moves like a silent movie newsreel: fast, herky-jerky, head down. It should be in black and white, with a guy in a derby, stage left, banging away on an old upright piano. Dubliners plow ahead: "the economy be damned, I've got things to do! Also, if I don't show up early and stay late, I may wind up hurrying along to the dole window." All that's missing for the complete vintage effect is trolley cars bowling down the avenue, scattering pedestrians like sheep in a country lane. Oh, wait, they have trolley cars, too.

There is also the odd sight of men in business suits on bicycles: dozens of them on Michael Collins-era bikes, pedaling like mad to avoid being flattened by the trolleys. I had a wild vision of one of them drawing a gun and shooting down a G-man. I really need to lay off the Liam Neeson movies before bed.

Speaking of which, my interest in Mr. Collins, the Irish patriot and revolutionary, has led me into some interesting conversations about the man, his times, and his legacy. During these chats with the locals the film *Michael Collins,* which starred the aforementioned Mr. Neeson, often came up. It was generally agreed that it was a good "fillum" but that it strayed from the historical record. It's also generally agreed that Neeson played his part well but that he wasn't as good as Brendan Gleeson's portrayal of Collins in the much lesser known film, *The Treaty*.

The real enthusiasm, however, was reserved for Mr. Neeson's co-star, Julia Roberts, in particular her attempts at an Irish accent. Actually, there is no such thing as an "Irish" accent, just as there is no such thing as an "American accent." There is a southern accent, a New York accent, etc. Similarly, there is a Dublin accent, which is much different from a Tipperary accent, which is nothing like a Cork accent—which is not of this planet.

"Oh, she was awful!" was the universal response, accompanied by a sour-milk expression. I enjoyed this so much that I always followed up with the sure-fire provocation, "How about when she sang?" Here the responses varied but were in the same vein and always entertaining:

"She sounded like a pig in heat."

"Like an Irish girl born in America and raised in Alabama."

"Complete shite."

"If I had a gun I'd've shot myself."

"I'd be after hanging myself if it had gone any longer."

"Oh, Jaysus, fockin' awful."

"Margaret Thatcher would have been better."

And my favorite:

"If she's from County Longford, I'm from County West Carolina!"

That last one was from a Dublin cab driver. Like cabbies the world over, they tend to have the most colorful language and memorable phrases. If you want to have fun while sitting in the never-ending traffic heading into Dublin from the airport, just ask how the commemorative Collins coins are selling. Julia will come up before you're off the M1, and after you've given up trying to pronounce "Baile Átha Cliath" (the Irish name for Dublin, meaning "town of the hurdled ford") in your head. Trust me, you'll never get it right and you'll just sprain your tongue and give yourself a headache.

Regarding Irish names for things, the Irish language is rich, deep, and boasts the oldest surviving vernacular in Western Europe. It is also extremely difficult to learn to speak and understand. Irish language courses (not "Gaelic," which refers to the group of dialects spoken in areas of Ireland, England, France, and Spain) are mandatory in the schools, and the language has made an incredible comeback considering the efforts made by the English over the course of 7 centuries to stamp it out but, except for some areas in the west of the country, it's rarely spoken. Grammar and spelling rules would help, but none are apparent. Letters that are complete strangers in every other language hang out together in Irish as the closest of friends. "Mb," "mh," "bh," the wild threesome "dhg," and my favorite, the linguistic orgy that is "mhfh," are often inseparable in Irish and always indecipherable to Americans and a good part of the Irish people. Attempts to remedy this can be found in language camps and immersion courses offered on both sides of the Atlantic. The best way for visitors to learn at least a few words is to read the road signs, which are usually displayed in both English and Irish. There you can see that "Tipperary" comes from "Tiobrad Arann," or "house of the well of Ara;" and "Kilkenny" from "Cill Chainnigh," "church of Cainnech." You're well on your way now, and should have no problem in the Gaeilge areas of the western counties, where Irish—Gaeilge--is the first official language. Well, except for around Dingle where the tourist trade feeds the year-round residents, who don't want their Euro-carrying visitors getting lost and winding up in Kerry because they couldn't read the signs.

A lot of Dublin looks like any other city. There is beautiful old architecture, to be sure, but too much of it was torn down when the powers-that-were decided to modernize the landscape with too much poured concrete molded in the House of Soviet Bloc style. The area around Merrion Square still boasts rows of Georgian-era townhouses with colorful doors and polished brass knockers (not to be confused with the knockers on the statue of Molly Malone, "the tart with cart"; cockles and mussels alive, indeed), but Dublin lost a bit of its old-world flavor in that regrettable spasm of 1970's Eastern Europeanism. Most tourists will only see, or care to see, the parts of Dublin that lay south of the river Liffey which divides the city in half. Except for a short stretch of O'Connell Street and perhaps Croke Park, north Dublin is ignored by the tourists, the locals, and the government. Its mostly working class residents don't care about your trip and don't want your company. In this they are no different than working class neighborhoods in America. They're much too busy trying to find a job or hang on to the one they have. In fact, except for a walking distance radius around south Dublin you'll miss most of the city. This would be a shame since, standoffish Northsiders aside, there is much to see outside of what you can cover without a bus or taxi. Some of these sights and sites are well-covered by the tourist trade folks. The Guinness brewery and Kilmainham jail both require a well-worth-it bus ride. They're also both easy to miss, so ask the driver to tell you when the stop is approaching and sit up front so you can hear him. "Up front" means "within arm's length of the driver." I discovered this when I sat with my son no more than 6 feet behind the driver and wound up on an empty bus at the end of line in an empty housing estate adjacent to an empty shopping mall. The Celtic Tiger ran out of gas well before the bus did, and these moonscape-like desolated areas are evidence of the overexuberance and unchecked optimism of the Irish during the '90's.

"I called out the stop, Yank. You must have been too far back," said the driver with a barely concealed smirk. Ah. A screw with the tourists type. They exist here, too.

"I'll sit closer next time," I replied. *Close enough to slap you in the back of the head*, I did not add. Oh well. We waited for the next bus.

"He'll be along in a few minutes," said the driver, still smirking, as he changed his sign to "out of service" and drove off—probably changing the sign to "Dublin City" once we was out of our view. My son and I settled in for a long wait. This wasn't our first time around and we both knew that "a few minutes," especially when it pertained to public transportation, meant anywhere from half an hour to "I give up, let's call a taxi."

We got to Kilmainham, which is not to be missed, and then the brewery, ditto. We also practically sat on the driver's lap on the way.

"We missed the driver's call on the way out," I said.

"Ah," replied the driver, "Skinny guy, with a face you'd like to push in?"

"Um..." says I. The driver smiled. "He does it all the time. Don't mind him, now, he's a sour one."

Back to the present. As I sipped and puffed away at O'Callaghan's, I was passed by a group of the cutest, most well-scrubbed, shy youngsters on their way to school. Pressed uniforms, starched shirts, and faces that light up at the slightest eye contact are enough to brighten the mood of even the worst wise-guy observer ... like me, for instance. They were the happiest humans on the street, which was especially remarkable because it was the beginning of the school year. I made a mental note to return in February, but I had every confidence that they would look just as neat, pressed, and happy then as when I first saw them. I've seen the same outfits on kids walking off to school in the Jamaican mountains and the sidewalks of the Bronx and they were just as clean, pressed, cheerful, and shy. Whatever the schools in these places are doing, they're doing it well—unless there's something in the starch I don't know about.

The adults were not as cheerful, as I've said, but even they would offer a decent "good morning" if I caught their eye, nodded, and smiled. For all its similarities to an American city at the beginning of the work day, Dublin was not Chicago and the reflexive friendliness of the Irish shone through at the slightest interaction with another human. I was struck yet again by the optimism of the country. Despite centuries of oppression, years of economic stagnation, and the recent collapse of the Celtic Tiger, the Irish are still a happy people. Sure, it's a stereotype, and sure, I've met my fair share of surly gripers, but it's true nonetheless. And even the surly ones will lose their grumpy-pants sourpuss looks when you buy them a pint and tell them how wonderful everyone's been to you.

Okay, so maybe this *is* a paean to Dublin. What can I say? The people here will probably always trump a bad economy, the murderous trolleys, and those hasty wrecking balls.

How to Pack for Ireland in Two Easy Steps

I've been fortunate enough to visit the Emerald Isle three times in the last four years. I'm returning in August to spend time with American ex-pat old friends, new Irish cousins, and the remaining 17 people on the island that I haven't yet met. I won't call myself an expert on Irish travel (well, not out loud, anyway), but I have learned a thing or two about how to keep the luggage down to no more than two bags and a carry-on and have all the pieces weigh less than the *Titanic*.

When packing for Ireland, there are two important things to remember:

> It's going to rain today.
> It's going to rain tomorrow.

Now, don't let this put a damper (har!) on your plans or your packing. Trust me, once the rain stops (and it will, very soon) and the sun comes out, you'll be in awe of the scenery before you can shake the drops off your jacket. The Irish sky after a soft rain is breathtaking. You can see for miles and miles, and the legendary shades of green for which Ireland is justly famous will total a lot more than just the 40 traditional shades.

That said, there is an Irish expression: "There is no bad weather, only inappropriate clothing." Herewith, my expert (whoops, did I say that out loud?) advice on how to pack, in two simple steps:

> Loosely pack one bag for the rain, and the sun that will follow.
> Loosely pack another bag for the sun, and the rain that will follow.

There now, wasn't that easy? Okay, maybe not. Allow me to elaborate. Packing for Irish weather can be summed up in one word: layers. T-shirts, light sweaters, a good waterproof—not "water-resistant"—jacket, a waterproof hat, and good walking/hiking shoes. Pack only outerwear that can be sprayed with a garden hose. Thinner is better. Sweaters and jackets should be thin enough to tie around the waist or stuff in a backpack. Undergarments made of moisture-wicking material are excellent: thin, lightweight, comfortable, and nothing that could give you a rash. I highly suggest hiking boots, rather than shoes, because once you leave the paved streets of Dublin you'll be wandering far and wee over tall grass, short grass, newly mown grass, bogs, streams, and country lanes. Slip into your good, cushioned-sole wool socks and off you go.

Now let's look closely at what I mean by "loosely." This is very important, as it will save you time, energy, and money, both while you're in Ireland and while you're at the airport departure counter crying over having to leave Ireland. You have to leave room in your bags for all the clothes you are going to purchase, to wit:

- the Trinity College hoodie from the souvenir shop in Grafton Street (and by the way: that T-shirt that proclaims how drunk you got in Temple Bar? Put it back. It's embarrassing. You'll understand why after a few days)
- that beautiful Donegal tweed cap
- the absolutely gorgeous shawl you get at the Avoca shop near the entrance to Killarney National Park
- the pink Wellies with the cute little sheep and shamrocks you will buy in Clare when the Skechers I told you not to pack get soaked in Doolin
- the Aran sweater for your brother-in-law
- the half-dozen other "ohmyGodIjusthavetogetthis" items that will fill your bag quicker than you can say "bodhran," which you'll have to check at the gate despite your strenuous objections

Don't worry: it will be fine. You think you're the first to buy all this stuff?

The advantages of packing this way will be evident as soon as you arrive at the rental car lot and discover exactly how compact a compact car is. You will find that your bags will actually fit into the space that those eternal optimists at Avis claim hold "4 to 5 pieces of luggage."

Packing tip #1: when you check into your room that first day, transfer your clothes to one bag and leave the other for purchases and well-bagged dirty laundry. This way, you're not rummaging through both bags looking for dry socks while destroying turf Christmas ornaments (which are very practical, as they're made from dried and pressed peat: you can burn them for warmth if times get really tough back home and you can't pay the electric bill due to throwing around those euro bills like the Monopoly money they so resemble), Belleek vases, and Waterford crystal. Aran sweaters are better than Styrofoam for cushioning.

Packing tip #2: although hard-case luggage is practical for reducing breakage, it's impractical for stuffing into a full hatchback. Just cushion the fragile stuff. Better yet, have it shipped. It will arrive in a week or so, like a gift to yourself from Ireland.

My family and I learned these lessons through trial and error, and when I leave for Ireland this summer I will go with one half-filled, soft-sided suitcase filled with a few shirts, a jacket, one sweater, my Donegal tweed cap (told ya!), and my big green Wellies (stuffed with Lycra/spandex undergarments) that I got in County Tipp after I stepped in . . . a substance . . . and ruined my Skechers.

I will leave at home my dressy clothes; Ireland is, as a rule, a very informal and relaxed place. Plus, there's this great little shop in Dingle Town that has the coolest European-cut dress shirts. I will also leave my "I Got Sh**-Faced in Shamrock Land" shirt in the bottom of my bureau drawer. It still has the tags on it.

I will take my passport, copies of my itinerary and contact information, wall plug adapters, extra memory cards, prescription meds, phone chargers (get an International Traveler Plan or buy an Eircom card upon arrival and save yourself some money), camera, batteries, and cigarettes. Cigarettes are frightfully expensive. Hopefully you don't smoke, but a great way to meet the locals is to stand outside with the nicotine fiends for the craic (or, as you might know it, fun). An offered Marlboro is a good icebreaker. Odd, but true.

Finally, when I get to the airport to go home, I will not have to pay for an extra, overweight, or oversized bag; my fragile items will be either well packed or in the capable hands of FedEx, and I will have no worries except how to keep the teardrops from ruining my boarding pass.

I wish you happy and safe travels, and if you're in Ireland this August, the first round is on me.

Once Upon a Time in Belfast

I was sitting on the sofa in my living room one fine evening, minding my own business, when my wife Cindy walked in and announced that another ("another"—I love saying that!) trip to Ireland was necessary. As I'm not one to argue with my spouse, I immediately agreed. "When should we go?" I asked.

"No," she replied. "Not us, just you. You need to go alone so you can play with your friends without having to keep me and Aeron [our son] entertained. Go wander around, see your friends, stay out late."

My wife laughed. I must have looked like a person who had just hit the lottery with a ticket he didn't know he had purchased. "Um…okay. Well…I'll see about flights." I left scorch marks on the carpet.

My plan was to spend most of my time in Co. Tipperary visiting friends I had made in our prior trips to my grandfather's land. I did want to take a day or two and see a few new places. As I'd had the great fortune to visit thrice before, there were not too many tourist sites left to see. We'd covered every county in the Republic. The North, however, was—except for Derry and the Giant's Causeway—undiscovered country.

Belfast! Capital city of the Northern Ireland statelet, home to famous linen and ships, and shorthand for the Troubles that had plagued the northern corner of the island for centuries. As the majority of my days would be spent in the middle of the island, I decided to visit Belfast first.

I landed in Dublin on a fine morning, bringing with me that big, bright, yellow ball of fire so seldom seen in the sky during this unusually wet Irish summer. I collected my expertly packed bag (see earlier in this work my discussion of "How to Pack for Ireland in Two Easy Steps"), picked up my rental car, and headed out of the lot towards the modern motorway for the scenic ninety-minute drive north. I negotiated the roundabouts without difficulty and veered onto the M1, merging into the lane behind a large truck. This is traditional. It immediately started to rain (this is also traditional). Not a sprinkling rain, nor a drizzle, but a deluge (ditto). I fumbled around for the proper controls (ditto ditto), activating turn signals, headlights, brights, fog lights, and the radio before finding the wiper switch. "Every time…" I muttered, mentally smacking myself for not learning my lesson (ditto).

As soon as I got the controls figured out, the rain stopped (dit—oh, never mind) and a glorious sun lit up some of the most spectacular scenery on the island. The views continued the entire way north. Good Lord, but I do love this place.

I had a reservation for one night at the Hotel Europa. The Europa is famous for a couple of things; one is having been the hotel of choice of President Clinton. The other is for being the most-bombed hotel in Western Europe (the hotel itself proudly proclaims this, by the way). Which is fame and which is infamy I'll leave to you, depending upon your politics. Mr. Clinton played a big part in the 1998 Good Friday Agreement that ended the violence, so I was very safe thanks in part to Bill—and by the way, well played, Bill. I also recommend the Europa for its very convenient location just off the well-signposted main motorway, which saved me the trouble of an unintended tour of the city and kept me from winding up on the ferry to Scotland.

The Europa has a convenient turnaround and I parked in front of the ornamented entrance, brought in my professionally packed bags, and stopped at the concierge desk. I was greeted by Head Concierge Martin Mulholland, President Les Clefs d'Or, "the Golden Key," which is a mark of excellence. Martin expertly handled my luggage, exchanged my car key for a valet ticket (off-site, £16 per day, and well worth it), and answered every question I posed with courtesy, patience, and a smile.

I checked in and got settled, then made a reservation with Billy Scott's Black Taxi Tour for a cruise around the Unionist and Nationalist neighborhoods. Having a few hours before the tour, I set about exploring the city. I had the obligatory tourist map but I also like to ask strangers for directions. It not only helps where the printed source may be incorrect or outdated but it's also a great excuse to talk to people. The locals have the usual set, serious faces of urbanites, but they lit up with genuine smiles when approached for guidance, and all were eager to give detailed directions. There were even a few who offered to walk me to my destination, and one who gave me his phone number and insisted I call him when I arrived.

I wandered around Belfast. City Hall is a beautiful edifice, festooned with ornate carvings, surrounded by lovely grounds and dotted with statues. Many of Belfast's buildings are decorated with interesting architectural details from various periods, and I whiled away a couple of hours until it was time for the Black Taxi tour.

I headed back to the Europa and was met by my driver and guide, Andy, a stocky gent with Popeye forearms and a disarming smile. He gave me a quick overview of the tour, we hopped in, and off we went.

Andy proved to be as knowledgeable as he was friendly, and by that I mean he knew everything. We made a dozen stops, with Billy explaining the meanings of the symbols, faces, expressions, and reasons for the murals that dotted the sometimes bleak cityscape of the Shankhill and Falls Road areas. The term "sectarian violence" is used all over the news for places all over the globe, but it hit me hard when I saw faces and names that could have come from my high school yearbook. I'll say no more about that except that it is a tour not to be missed and never to be forgotten. May they maintain the peace!

We completed the one-hour tour in just under two hours. I have some knowledge of the history of the Troubles, and Billy took me to places not normally seen so that I could be properly educated, all the while taking phone calls from his wife and assuring her that no, he wasn't at the pub and that yes, he'd be home soon. The £30 cost was nothing for such an experience and I gladly overtipped, traded sincere goodbyes with my guide, and headed off to the Crown Liquor Saloon—a bit shaken and with a new appreciation of some of the trials of the North.

The Crown Saloon is another spot not to be missed. It sits directly across from the Europa. If you want to see a classic, famous, historical, and simply gorgeous pub, come to the Crown. Pressed tin ceilings, cozy snugs, ancient memorabilia, and expert bartenders make the Crown the place to be for immersing yourself in traditional atmosphere. As with any pub in Ireland, some of the best money you can spend there will be buying a round for the locals nearest you and enjoying hours of conversation about anything and everything. The soft "Nordy" accent is simply musical. Before I knew it, it was after midnight and the pizza place just down a side street from the Crown was perfect for a take-away meal and a good night's rest prior to my morning appointment with the *Titanic*.

The Titanic Experience was another "must-see" recommendation from my friends in Irish tourism. Situated in the docklands area and completed to celebrate the 100th anniversary of the *Titanic*'s launching, the Titanic Experience is a multimedia wonder. Filled with artifacts and information, the self-guided tour (guided tours are also available) takes you through the history of Belfast, the nuts-and-bolts (literally) of the *Titanic*'s construction, and the details of her maiden voyage and fateful rendezvous with the iceberg. The tour is well laid out and courses smoothly though large exhibits, an amusement park–style gondola ride, and an excellent short film presentation.

I'd taken a taxi there in the morning; I decided to walk back to the hotel. McHugh's Pub is said to be the oldest in Belfast, serving pints since 1711. I passed City Hall, and the city's own version of the leaning tower of Pisa (you'll see). Back at the hotel, my time in Belfast was drawing to a close. Once again Martin showed his expertise and kindness in getting my car and bags collected. I left Belfast and headed towards Armagh and

Fermanagh, and my older friends in the Republic, but I already missed my new friends in the North and I regretted spending only one night. I hope to make this trip twice upon a time.

Why in the World Would He Leave?

My son Aeron stared out the window of our rental car as we drove north from Cashel. It was August 12, 2007, our first day in Ireland. I'd waited 42 years for this trip. My son only had to wait 8 years (which he never fails to remind me about—the lucky little...but never mind that). We were on our way to Thurles, and from there to Drumbane. Or Drombane. Or even Dromban. However one spelled it, that's whence we Britts came and that's where we were going.

We traveled along in silence for a bit, Aeron and my wife Cindy and me, just taking in the beautiful scenery under a sky like we'd never seen. Presently, Aeron said, "Daddy, why did your grandpa have to leave Ireland?"

Now that's an odd way to phrase it, I thought. I said, "What makes you think he had to leave?"

"Who would want to move away from here unless they had to?"

A fair question, and not an easy one to answer. "Well now," I said in my perfect Tipperary accent (which I later tried out on our hostess in Tipperary, who seemed to think I was from Brisbane—I never realized the two accents were so similar). "That's an interesting story." I settled back in my seat and tried to get comfortable, which was harder than it sounds, as I was on the wrong side of the road, the car, and the gear box, and just recently had experienced something called the "Red Cow Roundabout." I doubted that I'd ever really be comfortable in an automobile again.

"It was 1906," I began, "and John Francis Britt—my grandpa—was nineteen years old and the third oldest son of a farmer. Now being the third oldest meant that John Francis would not inherit the farm. It would go to his eldest brother Jerry—"

"Is that who you're named after?"

"No, I'm Gerard, he was Jeremiah."

Aeron looked disappointed. I quickly added, "But you know, now that I think about it, I seem to remember my father mentioning something about that, so maybe I am."

He looked happy again. "I bet you are."

Then he asked what I'd hoped he wouldn't. "Who am I named after?"

"Well now, that's another story. One story at a time." Hopefully I'd come up with something good. "Now where was I?"

"1906."

"Right, 1906, and John wasn't getting the farm, and who wants to live with his brother all his life? Can you picture me living with Uncle James?"

"Heck, no, you'd kill each other."

"That's right. So: John was nineteen, a bachelor. He was looking to make his fortune, find a wife, settle down, and start a family of his own. Now in those days, and in too many other days in Ireland, work was hard to find, and many, many people had to leave Ireland if they wanted any hope of a good life. In fact, that's what his brother Michael—the second oldest—had done in 1900. He'd packed up his things and took the boat to America. Now Michael was living in Brooklyn, where he'd found work as a blacksmith, gotten married, and had two children! Mick—that's what they called him—wrote to John and told him to come to America. Mick sent John a ticket for boat passage, and John left Ireland from a place called Cobh—except they had changed the name to Queenstown."

"Why did they do that?"

"Because the queen had landed there once."

"So what?" American boys are not much impressed by royalty, though that may just be his blood.

"They've changed it back since then."

"Good."

"So, with $25 of American money in his pocket, a healthy sum at the time, young John Francis Britt boarded the SS Etruria, bound for America and a new life. He arrived in New York on April 8 and stepped off the boat into an uncertain future. He was sad for the home he left behind, but he was determined to make the best of it in America."

"He did a good job, too."

"How do you know that?"

"Because he had your daddy, and your daddy had you, and you had me, and now I get to come back to his home. I bet he's happy we're back." I didn't reply.

"Dad?" I couldn't reply.

The sun is shining but I can barely see the road.

Get Me to the Islands, Seanie

One of the many things that fascinated me about Ireland was its monastic history. And the site that fascinated me most was Skellig Michael. Beehive huts? Puffins? Big chunk o' rock in the Atlantic? Sail on, child of Brendan!

While planning for our trip I had marked Skellig Michael on my tourist book map with a big "?" in orange hi-liter. That meant "love to see it, a bit expensive, we'll see." I was looking at it while my wife and son, per family agreement, packed up on our last morning in Kenmare. They packed and unpacked. I planned, drove, arranged, and guided. It worked out well.

As I stacked our bags by the front door of the Water's Edge B&B (I did the heavy lifting, too), I spoke to the owner about our plans and mentioned Skellig Michael. What followed paints an excellent picture of the Irish people.

Mrs. O'Shea went on about what a good idea that was, how only so many can go each day, we'll love it, and who did we make our reservations with? Um…well, see, there's this big orange question mark here.

"The boats only hold about a dozen people," she explained, "and there are only three or four boats that go each day." Ah, well, I thought, it was only a possibility anyway. Then Mrs. O'Shea proved that in Ireland, yes, all things are local: "But I know one of the boat drivers, Seanie. I'll give him a ring, maybe he's got room for you." Four boats a day from a distant port and my hostess knows one of them well enough to ring him up on short notice. Nice.

She came back from the kitchen. "Okay, Seanie said he's got room, but they may not go out today due to the water being a bit rough. High waves, he said. But if you want to go, he'll wait for you. You'll have to leave now, it's a bit of a drive." She gave clear and precise directions through town to the Portmagee Road. Three turns later I was already confused and pulled over to ask a couple of workmen for directions. My wife and I discussed the exchange all the way to the port:

Me: "Excuse me, good morning, could you tell me which road to take for Portmagee?"

Workman #1: "Hello, hello. Portmagee?"

Workman #2: "Portmagee? Which way do you want to go?"

Me: "Um..."

#1: "You'll want this road to the left, but you can take the other, too."

#2: "It depends on which way you want to go."

Me: "Um…whichever will get me there faster."

#1 & #2: "Oh, well in that case you'll want the road on the left."

Me: "How long is the drive?"

#2: "Oh, it's a good hour and half, at least."

#1: "At least."

I looked at my watch. 9:30. The boat left at 10:30.

Me: "Well, shoot, that's not good. We're trying to catch a boat to Skellig Michael and it leaves in an hour."

#1: "Oh, well in that case you can make it."

#2: "Just take the road on the left."

Me: "You think I can make it in an hour?"

#1: "If the boat leaves at 10:30, you can make it."

In Ireland, as I discovered then and after, time and distance are often relative to one's need. A 90-minute drive became an hour's drive because two workmen didn't want to disappoint a stranger. I thanked the men and pointed the rental car at the road on the left. As we pulled away, I could've sworn I heard one of the men call, "Tell Seanie we said hello!" But that may have just been my imagination.

We made the 90-minute drive in an hour, of course, despite my wife gasping every time we went around a bend. This was, for once, not due to my driving but to yet another incredible view. Tidal pools stretching out to our left, the deep browns contrasting with the lush greens of the banks. Dappled sunshine on hills and fields and sheep with red dots and sudden rain and cows and rock walls and stone cottage ruins and sheep with blue dots and horses and sudden sunshine and …

Suddenly we were in Portmagee, pulling right up to the concrete pier. A small boat gently rocked below iron rungs imbedded in the concrete. Someone obviously unfamiliar with the act was descending the rungs and was paused just above the boat as a man in full rain gear reached a hand up to help them. A few people sat in the boat, looking smug, while a few waited above, looking doubtful. This must be the place. I exchanged meeting plans with my wife and my son and I headed to the boat.

The group above the boat included another man in full rain gear. He looked quite relaxed, and I spoke to him. "Hi, I'm looking for Seanie."

"Are you Gerry?" he asked.

"I am."

"Ah, you made it, well done. I'm Seanie." I shook his hand, which felt like steel wrapped in sandpaper. "In you get, then."

In we got, then, my son scrambling down the rungs like he'd been doing it all his life and me just a bit less so. I declined the hand of the gent in the boat, thank you, sir, and managed to land without falling or pulling a hamstring, thank you, God.

Seanie boarded and handed us rain gear. "It'll be a bit wet," he said. "Put this on and sit down, we'll be off in a minute." He moved around the boat, casting off lines. We donned the cold, wet gear and sat on the bulkhead. I could feel the vibrations from the engine. The smell of diesel mixed with the damp air. The sun had disappeared and it was chilly.

Seanie stood before us. "Okay, could I have your attention for just a moment." Ah, the safety briefing, I thought. In America, this is the part where the captain gives us the estimated travel time, tells us what to do in case of emergency, and demonstrates the proper use of a life jacket. In Ireland, this is the part where Seanie says, "It's a bit rough out there today, so stay seated. You'll be getting wet." End of safety briefing. Seanie disappeared into the small cabin, opened the throttles, and off we went into gray Atlantic.

We watched the cove grow smaller as we cleared protected water. Then the waves got higher. Then it started to rain. Seawater sloshed over the deck and soaked our shoes. The rain came harder and the waves got higher. We were pelted by cold rain and freezing sea spray.

"You know," I said over the roar of the engine to a couple from Seattle who were on their honeymoon, "if we were back home we'd be warm and dry in an enclosed cabin, getting hot chocolate and t-shirts from the snack bar."

"I know," replied the bride, "Isn't this great?"

The groom added, "If we were back home we'd still be at the pier getting the safety briefing. I like this better." Judging from the smiles of our fellow soaked travelers, so did they.

I won't say more about the journey except that, when it was over, we were all wet, cold, tired, and absolutely exhilarated. It is an experience not to be missed.

And tell Seanie I said hello.

The Boys of Ballyfinnane

It was our third trip to Ireland, and my family and I planned to take a whole week to stay in the Upperchurch-Drombane area of County Tipperary, home of my grandfather's family. After landing in Dublin on a Friday and staying the weekend in Kildare with an old friend from New York, we made our way to the village of Upperchurch.

We had rented a small cottage in Dooree Commons, just up the road from the village. 'Up the road' meaning a few miles in this particular case. I had directions to the place from the cottage's owner, but I stopped into a pub in the village to check—it wouldn't do to take a wrong turn and wind up in County Sligo. Four young men at the bar in Ryan's greeted me, with one of them saying, by way of hello, "Ain't you the big fella! I like a challenge!" Now, I'm a veteran of the gentle ribbing that you get in Irish pubs, so I counted them aloud and kindly pointed out that four of them against one of me was hardly a fair fight, and perhaps he should run home and get a few more friends.

"That's the talk!" he laughed. "What brings ya here?" I told him where I was going, and he barely opened his mouth before an old gent at the bar interrupted and gave me detailed directions, which turned out to be nearly, but not quite, correct. What's an extra turn between friends? After a few dead ends at cattle gates, we found it—mostly by accident—our quaint old cottage built in 1905, featuring a lovely fire stove with a supply of turf stacked nearby. It was two-level, with a bedroom, shower, kitchen, and sitting room on the main level. Upstairs held another two bedrooms with soft beds tucked under the eaves. Heaven. My teenage son claimed an upstairs room and my wife and I unpacked in the main level.

Once we were settled, I headed back up to the village with my son for supplies. We stopped in at O'Dwyer's grocery-slash-post office-slash-undertaker and chatted a bit with Mrs. O'Dwyer while we gathered our purchases of fresh brown bread and butter, milk and eggs, and ham and cheese. I stashed the box of goods—no plastic bags here—in the hatchback.

We hopped in the car and drove 100 yards to the community center at the other end of the village. Here we spoke to Nuala Ryan, the centre's administrator, about our plans to wander Upperchurch and Drombane, attend a hurling match, and discover where my grandfather spent his youth before he left for America in 1906.

Like so many other Irish Americans, I've spent hours on genealogy websites poring over census and land records hoping to uncover information that might get me closer to the actual piece of land that was home the Britts (or Bretts—Irish names changed spellings like divas change gowns).

Nuala directed me to Paddy Kinnane's Pub, where the owner, the wonderful Niamh, provided me with names, numbers, and directions to a variety of sources. Niamh also said something that was music to my ears: "You look like the Britts of Drombane, especially around the eyes."

Her sister Siobhan appeared with coffee, tea, cakes, and cookies and I told them the facts as I knew them. Both ladies agreed that my conclusions were correct and that a visit to the local historian would most likely bear definitive proof. Thus fortified by this good news, Aeron and I left the pub with a promise to return later in the evening with my wife. We drove back to the cottage. Cindy had been busy getting everything in its place and Aeron and I put the groceries away. I told Cindy about my conversations in the village. After a snack of bread and butter and tea, I insisted on trying out the stove and, after only a few false starts, the cottage was filled a small amount of smoke but a large amount of the sweet smell of burning turf.

By this time we were all ready for a real meal, so back we went to Kinnane's. Siobhan's son Fergal—big, bald, scary, and friendly—led us to a table set for three around a cozy nook near the just-lit turf fire. Heaven, continued.

We sat on a soft, cushioned, and embroidered banquette and chatted with our hosts for a while. Every now and then I'd peer over Fergal's shoulder, which is not an easy task because his shoulders are the size of the Wicklow Mountains, and tried to count the patrons at the bar. There looked to be eight or ten. I had in mind something I'd always wanted to do, and I did some mental math. "Fergal, if it wouldn't be too vulgar or presumptive, I'd like to buy a round for the house. Would anyone mind?"

Fergal took a quick look over his shoulder. "That crowd?" He laughed. "No, I'd say they wouldn't mind at all. Come on, I'll introduce you."

It turned out to be the best money I've ever spent—an investment that would provide me with song and conversation worth their weight in gold and, as it turned out in the months and years to come, good friends. Brian the stucco worker sang a sad "Michael," about slain leader Michael Collins, and I returned the favor with a bit of Sinatra. We harmonized (badly) to Johnny Cash, and I returned to my table for a wonderful steak dinner with broccoli and boiled potatoes, and cauliflower and mashed potatoes, and carrots and fried potatoes, and mixed greens and roasted potatoes, all in portions that could have fed an entire hurling team.

After dinner I retired to the outdoor smoking area and was soon joined by other bar patrons, who introduced me to the finer points of "slaggin'," otherwise known as "takin' the piss," otherwise known as "let's see what the Yank tourist is made of." I was treated well and given only a light verbal lashing, partly because I took it with good grace and partly because I can spit out great curse words with a decent Irish accent.

"You're all right, Yank."

That night in the pub was a memorable one. I was eager for another, but I was determined to keep things moving on the research front and not stay up 'til all hours and sleep until same. And so, after a hearty breakfast of eggs, rashers, and brown bread, I left my family to wander the local lanes and, through prior arrangements made by my pub hosts, made my way down to the village of Drombane and the home of Eugene Short, the local historian and keeper of the record books.

Drombane is called a village only because there's no other word for a place so small. It's really just a spot at the cross of two small lanes that lead nowhere except to other small lanes which in turn, at some point, lead to roads big enough to take you somewhere else. There is a pub. It's a bit hard to find due to renovations but, like most village pubs, well worth the effort. Diagonally across from the pub is a community hall. A small and beautiful Catholic church sits across it. Next to the church is small shop with a single petrol pump. 50 yards in any direction will lead you to nothing more than a few small homes, a couple of Gaelic games pitches, and more horses than people. It is peaceful, quiet, and, to a harried American, a small slice of heaven.

There weren't many people moving about, but the ones I spoke to were very nice to me. They all knew the Britt name and asked as many questions about me as I did of them. I heard about relatives in America, how to actually get into the pub, Mass times, the upcoming dance at the hall next Friday evening, and that I should speak to Eugene about my family history.

I found Eugene's home with little trouble—meaning that I only passed it three times before daring to pull in and knock with any confidence that I had the right place. I was greeted by Eugene and his wife, along with a big, happy, main dog and a smaller yet just as happy back-up dog. There was also a pot of tea and a big slab of chocolate cake.

This was Ireland, so it was a while before we got down to opening books or looking at names. Once we had covered when we had arrived, where we were staying, how long we were staying, where we had been, where we were going, who we had met, who we had not met, and what we thought of the area, Eugene and I retired to his study to see if what I had in my files made any sense.

Eugene pulled a number of thick binders down from the shelf and placed them on a desk. "Now, Gerry," he said, "let's see if we can't locate your grandfather."

We sat and I showed him what I had concerning names and dates, my historical sources, what I was confident about and what I could reasonably deduce. I admitted that there were gaps that could mean I was mistaken, and that I was ambivalent about seeing his records for fear of discovering that I was in the wrong county. However, between his files and mine, we verified that my hours and months and years of searching were not in vain! I had the right family, the correct dates, and now, oh my God…even the exact house where my ancestors lived. A feeling of relief and a sense of completion overwhelmed me.

Eugene gave me directions to a tiny piece of land just south of Drombane village called Ballyfinnane, and the next morning I set out with my family from Upperchurch, left at the Newport Road, right at Fahy's Petrol, over the metal bridge, left at the tee, up and around and over narrow rutted lanes bordered by high hedges, avoiding potholes that could swallow my egg-like rental car, down into Drombane village, left at the still under renovation pub, past the stables and football pitch, left the junction and then a quick right, first right again, over the stone bridge, then finally a right down a short lane hidden among the hedges.

And there it was.

It was stucco-walled, shingle-roofed, with a small graveled front yard, a trash fire pit, a couple of small sheds and storage structures, and an acre of grass that may have been a paddock but was now empty. There was no one home—the last Britt, Peg, had died a few years ago and the house was now inhabited by persons unknown. We wandered about, my wife taking photos and me turning on the spot with my video camera.

When I was sure we had a visual record of every inch of the property, I called to my son and together we climbed the fence into the field. We walked a few yards in silence. I reached over and took his hand. He was fourteen and much too old to be holding his father's hand, but he didn't say a word. I told him to look around, breathe the air, feel the grass and the breeze and the sunshine. Remember it. The story is complete and he can tell it to his children, and to their children.

I wanted to tell him how much it meant to me that he was with me, but my throat was too tight. I wanted to look at him, but my eyes were too wet. I put my arm around his shoulder and held him close as we walked. I didn't want him to see his father blubbering. But he saw, and he knew.

We walked over tall grass and through bramble and bushes. Deep breaths. Drink it in. Finally, when there was no more to see and no more to say, we walked back to the drive and piled into the car. As my wife and son got buckled and settled in, I went still.

"Just a minute," I said, "I'll be right back." I climbed out the car and walked back to the gate.

"You done good, John Britt," I whispered. "You made it to America and we've made it in America. You have a good, beautiful, and smart great-grandson who I know you would love. Thank you for your courage; we'll always honor it with our own."

After a minute, I wiped my eyes and cleared my throat and turned back to the present. Aeron had stepped out of the car. My son was smiling at me. My son. The boy from Ballyfinnane.

The Hounds of Bandon (And Other Irish Beasts)

After two lovely nights at a B&B in Ballinadee (roll that softly over your tongue!), taking in the sights and sounds of pretty Kinsale, we loaded our bags and ourselves in the Renault and pointed the rental in the general direction of Kenmare. We were in no hurry, which is a good thing to be if you prefer to keep off Ireland's bigger roads. American ideas of time and distance are best left at the Hertz counter.

I followed our hostess's directions perfectly and we only passed the same church twice before I found the right road. My wife for some reason held a differing opinion of my performance and offered me the map.

"Put that away," I commanded. "I know exactly where I'm going."

After passing the same field so often that we were on a first-name basis with the cattle, I found the road to Bandon. "See?" I said, "I knew where I was going." My wife and son nearly pulled muscles rolling their eyes. I made the correct right turn from the correct left lane and on we traveled.

It's difficult enough remembering to keep your right elbow over the middle of road without the Irish countryside distracting you at (literally) every turn. I was admiring a particularly fine hill when I was forced to brake, quickly, for what had to be the largest pack of hounds ever assembled. They were suddenly everywhere: barking, baying, trotting, weaving, sniffing, looking, bumping, wagging—all in ceaseless motion and now surrounding our car, sticking their snouts in the window, sniffing my hand and face and, I'm sure, the spilled coffee, black bread, and rashers that were now strewn everywhere.

We could do nothing but laugh. "Dogs?" I protested. "It's supposed to be sheep! All the guide books have sheep in the road. No one said anything about dogs."

My wife struggled to find the find the window button. She likes dogs, but from a few feet away—and one at a time. My son talked back to the dogs, baying and barking and sticking his head out the window. We exchanged waves and greetings with the two herders who were waving the insanely happy canines around our car like a stream around a stone. What fun!

Later in the week we stayed in Doolin, Co. Clare for a few days. Doolin is a great base for trips to the Cliffs of Moher, the Burren, and even up to Mayo. We were on our way back from a Burren circuit when we stopped to watch the sun set over the ocean. No sooner had we sat on the roadside wall when my son said, "I see two donkeys!"

"Where did you hear that horrible term?" I demanded.

He pointed to our left. "Two donkeys!" Sure enough, two donkeys came strolling up the otherwise deserted beach like lovers on the strand, not 10 feet from us. This wasn't in the books, either. Up they came for a sniff, and I wondered if I still smelled of rashers. We all got a good look at each other, decided that none of us were a threat, and then the pair wandered off. My wife and son and I exchanged bemused looks, and then we all laughed until we were gasping for breath. Well, I thought, it's a beautiful enough sunset to share.

On our trip the following year, we attended mass at the church in Holycross, a beautiful old building of wooden beams and ancient stone. In the dark and cool, our steps echoed off the stone floor and the priest had only to whisper to be heard. After the service we lingered outside, talking to some parishioners. My son (again): "Um, Dad? I think I have new friends." I turned (again) to see two gigantic Irish wolfhounds nose to nose to nose with Aeron, sniffing and wagging and licking, apparently overjoyed to say hello to someone their own size. I looked at my wife.

"No," she said, reading my thoughts and smiling. "I don't think this is in the guide books, either. But it should be!"

Village dogs are a special breed. They require no leash, nor would they tolerate one. Rarely will you see a collar. They have owners in the nominal sense, but rural dogs are not pets in the American sense. They're members of the community, with all of the rights and privileges enjoyed by their human neighbors. They wander around, stopping here and there to say hello, give a sniff, get an ear scratched, and maybe score a sausage or rasher. You'll see them lazing in front of the grocer's in the morning, dodging killer tractors in the afternoon, and hanging out with the smokers outside the pub in the evening. There's contentment in the lazy wag of their tails.

Outside the villages you will encounter the farm dog. Farm dogs are work dogs. They have very little free time but are happy to take a few moments to greet any visitors to their land by charging at them full-speed while barking like mad. Fear not, for they will, invariably, go from 100-miles-an-hour to a full stop in about ten feet. The barking will stop and they will proceed to sniff every inch of your body that they can reach. Petting them is impossible. They'll dart away and nose-dive into another personal crevice. Your (human) host will attempt to wave the excited beast away, but he won't really put much effort into it. It's not that he enjoys watching you get nasally frisked (though he might be. I've seen more than a few poorly-hidden smiles during scenes like this), he simply knows it won't do any good. The dog will stop once he's satisfied that you aren't there to steal the sheep nor give him food.

In contrast to the village dog, who is usually of indeterminate parentage, the farm dog is more likely to be a pure-bred. Border collies are popular on Irish farms. Like all farm dogs they like to chase and bark at visitors. Like some farm dogs they also like to chase and bark at passing cars. But I've only seen border collies play chicken with traffic. There you are, driving down some rural road (no line down the middle), minding your own business, when—pop!—out darts a collie from the hedge. And before your brain can get your foot off the gas and on the brake he's gone—pop!—back into the hedge.

The first time this happened to me I assumed the dog just didn't see me coming. But after a few instances I started to check my rear view mirror. Sure enough, they were doing it with every passing car. I don't know if it's in the breed or if they just don't have enough work to do, but it's another reason to be careful on Irish roads.

Dogs aren't the only beasts one will encounter on the roads, of course. "Irish rush hour," a picture showing sheep causing a traffic back-up, is as popular a postcard as Blarney Castle. And this happens, for sure. What isn't shown on the postcards is the sheep as bully. A road will often cut through a sheep pasture, with no fencing or guard between grass and blacktop. Sheep eating on the left, how pretty. More sheep eating on the right, lovely. But why is there one sheep that insists on standing…right. In the middle. Of the road.

Just staring at you.

Acres of grass to his left. Acres more to his right. But he just stands there. Staring with those too-human eyes, silently mocking. Creeping up on him won't work, he knows you won't actually hit him. Nor will going around him work since the road is invariably too narrow. Forget tapping the horn. No, the only way to get that bully of a sheep off the road is to try to take his picture. Then he's gone. I swear they know exactly what they're doing.

Urlingford

While tracing my ancestry I spent most of my time working on my paternal grandfather's family. There was more information with which to start because my father had also worked on our genealogy when I was around 10 years old, though most of it vanished when he did. Having succeeded in finding my grandfather's information, and having exhausted all available sources, I turned my attention to what had always been something of a forbidden subject in my family: my paternal grandmother's past.

Unlike my grandfather, who died in 1925 at the age of 39, Nanny Britt lived to be 85. That said, she died in 1970 when I five years old so I don't have any memories of her either, but my older siblings remember asking her about Ireland and her youth. According to them, Nanny's only response was a terse, "We left Ireland, we're Americans now, and that's the end of it."

Although this was very disappointing, I knew that her attitude was not uncommon among immigrants around the turn of the twentieth century. Nanny—a.k.a. Helen Britt, née Holohan—arrived from Co. Kilkenny in 1903. Immigrants were eager for acceptance and did their best to assimilate quickly, often downplaying their foreign past in favor of their American future. In many cases the past was not a happy place. A history of poverty and hard times was forgotten, not celebrated. At least until better fed and educated children complained about their lives, that is.

At any rate, when researching my grandfather's history, I found a good amount of information about my grandmother. I discovered her birth year and place from US censuses, her year of immigration, and that she was a naturalized citizen.

The amount of information gathered by the census taker varied. One showed only her country of birth; another listed the specific place, Urlingford.

I discovered that Urlingford leans against the border of Co. Tipperary and even reaches into that county for a few hundred yards. The town is not too far from my grandfather's home in Drombane, Co. Tipperary, which made me wonder if my grandpa and grandma knew each other before emigrating. Grandpa Britt came over three years after her, in 1906. It's a widely held belief that Irish immigrants tended to cluster by county in ethnic neighborhoods. Research has proved this to be less true than commonly believed but, like other immigrant groups, relatives would more often than not live close to those who came before, making use of housing, employment, and church connections.

My grandparents had enough in common that the idea of their acquaintance prior to emigrating is not that far-fetched. Both had mothers whose family name was Ryan, they lived less than 50 miles apart in Ireland (albeit in turn of the century Ireland, where 50 miles may as well have been 500, transportation being what it was) and they lived near each other in New York. These common factors may have played a hand in their meeting, in either Ireland or New York. Ghetto myths aside, it was true that the Irish often socialized and formed friendships with those who came from the same region or county. Perhaps it was a social for folks from Co. Tipperary which might have gotten a look-in from some Kilkenny border families, or a chance meeting in s pub and a friendly conversation. Oh, Tipp is it? Urlingford, here. My niece's christening is Sunday—stop by. Such are the things that legends and family stories are made of.

So the sources I have for my one grandparent were copied and placed in the file for another. With a decent starting point, I then turned my attentions to finding information about Helen's Urlingford years. This proved to be a bit difficult due to one of the major frustrations of amateur genealogists: spelling.

How does one spell "Holohan"? Well, let's see. There's Holohan, Holahan, Holohon, Halohan, and Houlihan (for starters), and you can double that by adding a nice confusing O' at the front of each version. Didn't the census takers in Ireland in 1901 ask for the proper spelling? Maybe. Didn't the residents give them proper spelling? Same answer. Perhaps the census taker was from Dublin and didn't quite catch the vowels. Perhaps he "knew" how to spell their name and never asked. Perhaps the occupant didn't trust anyone from the Crown with a pen and paper, nosing around, asking questions.

My great-grandfather managed to age 15 years between 1901 and 1911, while his wife aged a mere 8. Was he lying? Was she, and to whom? Maybe the missus was keeping up a lie she first told on a date. Maybe she was recently vain. Maybe he didn't know, or care.

And perhaps great-grandpa had a reason to be evasive. Mistrust of English administration was a perfectly legitimate reason to dissemble, dissuade, and misinform. The Irish have long memories, and the past is always present. Any visit from the representatives of the crown was suspect. An official working for the foreign crown asking who's here today could lead to an official deciding who's gone tomorrow, without any good reason—or any reason at all for that matter.

A grown man in 1901, in that rural part of Ireland, would have been raised by parents with a deep and abiding resentment towards anything to do with the occupying government. Even my phrasing in this writing reveals an historical prejudice ingrained in my family DNA. Memories are long and they travel well.

After closely looking at and charting Nanny's information, I discovered a couple of things. One was that from the looks of things, no one knew how to spell her name, including her. However, I was able to narrow it down to H-o-l-o vs. H-o-l-a. The other thing was that she was definitely born in 1888. Or 1885. Or 1886. The woman's age changed every five years. This was true in both Ireland and America. Was it vanity? Did she fill out the marriage papers? Maybe John filled out the marriage papers in New York. Maybe he was home for the census. Putting the Saturday paper aside—who's this now?—and strapping on his suspenders as he opens the door. Census man, is it? Well, there's the three of us. Maybe the census taker was tired, worn out from climbing stairs and knocking on doors and crying babies and these immigrant Irish with accents thicker than molasses. Harried mothers with one on the hip, another tugging at her dress, and two more fighting in the kitchen. What's that? I'm sorry, hold on—will ya both shut yer gobs in there!

Whatever the reason, such is the fog that settles around our ancestors and forces a shift away from solid fact and into deduction and determination. Based on all I know, what is the most likely answer? The census is suspect; questions answered in haste must be viewed with that in mind. On the other hand, any request for that same information would more likely be accurate if the request was made in the course of an application for citizenship.

Having narrowed down the possibilities, but unable to move confidently forward, I came at it from the other direction. A search of the invaluable 1901 and 1911 Irish censuses revealed a number of Holohans in Urlinghford but, thankfully, no Holahans.

I'd like to go on to say that one lead led to another and that there was a joyous and tearful family reunion. There was not. I'd even like to say that the 1901 census revealed Nanny's family. It did not. The search continues, but I can certainly get the flavor of Nanny's town by walking its streets and lanes and visiting with its people.

So I did.

I'd landed in Dublin a few days before and had spent them with my ex-pat friend and his family in Kildare. Now I was on my way to the old Britt homestead in Tipperary, and Urlingford was an easy detour off the M8 towards Thurles. Through the roundy-round (my wife's term for what others call roundabouts), through another roundy-round, and into Urlingford.

Like so many small Irish towns and villages (those being terms of entity and not size, by the way), Urlingford is not much more than a pretty main street, perhaps a mile long and bookended by petrol stations. A smattering of estates, a national school, of course a church (or two or three), and beautiful farms, land, and rock walls as far as the eye can see. There is the requisite Gaelic Athletic Association (GAA) field on the road into town and assorted shops and pubs line both sides of (yes) Main Street.

As I said, it's not much different than many other small towns I've visited, except for one jarring sight. Urlingford, as I said, squats on the eastern border of Co. Tipperary and Co. Kilkenny. In sports-crazed Ireland, the hurling rivalries are fierce, but the Premier County and the Cats have a special dark place in each other's hearts. Before important GAA matches (hurling especially), flags and streamers and banners and signs are hung from every home and business. They are as good as signposts for marking a county border, and those unfortunate souls living in one county but rooting for another almost always choose discretion over valor and tend to keep their loyalties to themselves, or at least away from the windows.

So it was very odd to see dozens of black-and-amber Kilkenny flags hanging in windows, right alongside other windows festooned with the blue and yellow of Co. Tipp. What the …?

I continued down Main Street, marveling at the symmetry. I saw opposing colors hanging in every door and window, strung between neighboring houses and attached to every car antenna. This was either one very understanding or one seriously warring town, and I must admit (rather sheepishly) that I was ambivalent about which I preferred. Camaraderie and sing-alongs are wonderful, but I do love a good argument. Especially between hurling fans. And even more especially between Tipp and Kilkenny fans. Either way, a stop at a pub seemed appropriate in order to find out more.

I nosed into a spot near the Tipp end of town and strolled back along Main Street. A man stepped out of Molly Mac's Pub ahead of me for a cigarette. He was having trouble with his matches and I offered my lighter. This is how two hour conversations get started in Ireland. I don't promote smoking, but with indoor smoking banned almost everywhere on the island (the Bogside artists' studio in Derry being a notable exception), it does provide an excellent setting for a short conversation ("a short conversation" meaning anywhere from the time it takes to finish the cigarette to, oh, all night).

"Top o' the mornin' to ya," I said. No, I didn't. It would sound as silly as a visitor to the United States greeting everyone with a highly accented "Howdy, pardner!" A common greeting in Ireland is, "How are you?" It's akin to "How are you doing?" in the U.S., and slurred just as much. Howwaya. Hahyadoin. It's a bit contagious, actually, and each time I visit I fall into the habit more quickly. On this trip it popped out at the rental car counter. I wish I could hear myself with Irish ears. Or maybe not.

Just like in the U.S.—and everywhere else in the world, for that matter—the weather is always a good conversation starter in Ireland, especially in rural areas where it really does matter. And while the top-o'-the-mornin' stuff is certainly a false stereotype, the Irish talent for conversation is not. I once sat for an hour, enraptured, with four farmers in Drombane while they discussed the effects on the hay from all the rain. Every aspect was raised and dissected, with the men leaning over to explain to me, sotto voce, some fine point or other to make sure I was engaged and able to properly follow the conversation. The Irish are good at this. One particular conversational trait I've noticed is the habit of asking someone a question, particularly about something the questioner cannot possibly know the answer to, and then not accepting the answer. How long were you in hospital, Pakie? Ten days. No, you weren't!

It was a beautiful day in Urlingford, a rare thing that wet summer, and I said so. He agreed. I said Urlingford was a pretty town. He agreed with that, too. He asked where I was from. When I told him I was from Virginia, he said the most beautiful words I'd ever heard: "You don't look like an American." I took that as a compliment. What do I look like? "You look like an Irishman. Sound like one, too." I've never been in love with a man, but I came close just then. I wondered if he worked for the Tourist Board. Maybe they sprinkle people around the country to tell the crazy Yanks what they're dying to hear. Well, in addition to "It's not going to rain today," of course.

We smoked and talked. No, I've been here a few times. Yes, my grandmother. Holohan, do you know it? He did. He knew where all the Holohans lived in my Nanny's day, where they live now, and how to get there. Just down that road there. I've said this before, but it bears repeating: "just down the road" can mean 10 yards or 10 miles. No one wants to let you down by telling you exactly how lost you are. You just made a wrong turn. (I won't lead you on; there's no family reunion in this story. I am, however, working on one for August of this year. Sorry.)

My new friend's name was Steve and he accepted my offer of a drink, so we crushed out our butts on the wall receptacle and went into the dim coolness of Molly Mac's. This is Gerry Britt from America, he's part of the Holohans from down the road. I wasn't exactly sure which Holohans I was part of, but Steve assured me, and the other six patrons in the bar all agreed, that it was indeed them. Beats any census form, far as I'm concerned. That was enough to get the craic started. Everyone discussed Holohans. I was quizzed (but not contradicted, alas; still a tourist) about everything. I talked some, listened more, and had a grand old time.

After a while I felt comfortable enough to ask how the town managed the dueling county partisanship. "We try to be kind to the mentally defective," said one wag, a Tipp supporter.

"Who do you favor?" asked the barman.

"I favor buying a round before I answered," I replied. This went over well, as did my perfect equivocation of admitting to being a Tipp fan, "but with certain new feelings of allegiance as of right now."

"I told you he sounded like an Irishman, didn't I now!" gushed my hero, Steve.

"Yeah, he sounds just like you: full of shite," offered the Cat jersey–clad Mary with a snort and a smile.

I mentioned that Drombane jerseys look just like Kilkenny jerseys. Which brought up my grandfather, which conjured questions about him and his family, which led to another lively discussion about where the Britts lived then, where they live now ("Don't tell me they're in Ballingarry, because I've never met one"), who has them in their family, and why. Padraig (pronounced paw-rig, or pah-drig, or sometimes paw-rik, or not) the barman caught my eye and rolled his own.

"Are they always like this?" I asked.

"It comes and goes." He inclined his head toward me. "Some of it's for you. You're a new audience."

"Doesn't take much, then, does it," I said. He rolled his eyes again.

"Any reason for this bunch o' bollocks."

I raised my glass in their direction. "Any reason to do a thing is a good enough reason if you like doing it."

Padraig smiled, shook his head, and turned from the bar. "Jaysus, you do sound like an Irishman. Here, Gerry. I've a tune on the box for you." He held up a Euro coin over his shoulder.

"Ah, Jayus, Paddy, the man didn't come in to hear your songs!" called Steve. This made the bunch forget the Britts and immediately take sides on the music issue. Padraig dropped the coin in the jukebox, punched a few buttons, and made his way back to the bar.

"The man's got family in Tipperary, now, and this is a beautiful Tipperary song. Do you know it, Gerry? 'Goodbye Tipperary'?"

This was greeted with a chorus of assent as the music started. I'd never heard it, but when I did I was sorry I had missed it for so long. I discovered later that like so many Irish tunes, its lyrics varied. Here's the version I heard:

> *The ship it sails in half an hour*
> *To cross the broad Atlantic.*
> *My friends are gathered on the pier*
> *With grief and sorry frantic.*
> *My portmanteau is stowed below*
> *On the good ship Dan O'Leary;*
> *The anchor's weighed and the gangway's up*
> *I'm leaving Tipperary.*

The last line was sung in a suspiciously happy tone which made me laugh, especially since they were grinning at me and raising their glasses. And the chorus:

> *So goodbye, Mick, goodbye Pat,*
> *Goodbye Kate and Mary.*
> *The anchor's weighed and the gangway's up*
> *I'm leaving Tipperary.*
> *And now the steam is blowing off*
> *I can no longer stay.*
> *I'm bound for New York City, boys,*
> *Three thousand miles away.*

Grins and toasts, and maybe I got a bit misty-eyed at those last few lines. God, what a great song!

Everyone knew the first verse and the chorus, but accuracy fell off in the second verse and the third verse was mostly drowned out by everyone telling everyone else that they had the lyrics wrong and singing their own version all the louder.

> *I'm bound for New York City, boys,*
> *Three thousand miles away.*

"Now that's a Tipp song for ya."

"Are there any Kilkenny songs?" I asked. "I'm coming to it later than I did Tipp, but I'm as much a part of here," I waved to indicate the town, "as I am of there," pointing down the road to County Tipperary.

In the quiet after the song ended, Mary started off with something low and slow and everyone joined in better than before. "Better" meaning that no one really knew the lyrics but made up for it by singing louder and faster with each verse and laughing like eejits.

I looked at Paddy, who was murdering the tune like a champ—I found out later it was called "The Kilkenny Song" and is a popular drinking tune—and asked him if this was for me, too.

"A bit, yeah," he said, and then winked. "But they've been in here for a while, so don't let it go to your head."

Too late.

The Euro Considered, or, I'm Putting a Hotel on Marvin Gardens

I've been to Europe (okay, Ireland, but it still counts and I like saying "I've been to Europe") four times now, with a fifth trip in a few weeks. I have in my pocket, so to speak, 75 days of experience with the euro. The bills are beautiful; multicolored paper of various sizes and designs adorned with the faces of the great and famous, who look on approvingly as I pass them over the seat to the cabbie, over the bar to the publican, and over the Atlantic when I try to dig camera batteries out of my pocket at the Cliffs of Moher.

Ah, well. It's no big deal. What was that, a fiver? What are the pink ones again? Did I collect $200 when I passed Go? I don't know if the designers of the euro bills had American tourists in mind when they settled on these bills, but if so they are evil geniuses. To an American, a Euro bill looks like play money. Which, in a way, it is. To us, money is green. Money is never pink. If an American sees pink in a wallet, it means he has to go pick up his pants from the dry cleaners. Blue is not money, either. In fact, there is no blue paper in the United States. There used to be, when receipts were hand-written on blue pads, with carbon paper (ask your grandparents) underneath. You could buy a freezer's worth of food and list every item on one receipt. These days, you buy a gallon of milk you get 12 inches of receipt, two coupons, a bonus point voucher, and tickets to the Big Apple Circus at the fairgrounds. But I digress. Blue money means only one thing to me: the $50 bill in Monopoly.

This is the overriding sense, the lasting impression, that holding euros brings: I have a pile of Monopoly money to spend on anything I want. It doesn't matter! This *paper* isn't real money. Look at this one! It's tiny! It has an odd feel, like the tag on a mattress. And no matter how hard I try to keep them folded, once over, neatly in my pants pocket, I always wind up with a bill wadded into the bottom of my pocket like an old tissue, possibly used.

Don't get me wrong; I travel on a budget just like almost everyone else. But even after 75 days of practice, I still find myself at shop counters hearing numbers but not equating the words "seventeen fifty" with "twenty-four fifty U.S. dollars." I simply fish a ... what color is this? mauve? taupe? piece of paper out of my pocket (scattering coins that got caught up in the bills when they collapsed into a wad five minutes after I tucked them away) and blithely passing it over. Here you go. One mauve one for you, and I get back two-fifty in ... subway tokens?

Oh yeah, I forgot: no ones. Americans are conditioned to reach into their wallet for any purchase over 75 cents. Oh, you'll find the odd duck (read "female," because a man will never do it) who'll dig out $4.75 in quarters, but your average American pays in bills then throws the change in the car ashtray. As a result, if I don't consciously try to use the one- and two-euro coins, by the end of the day I end up shuffling down the street like a condemned man walking the last mile in manacles, my pockets bulging like ballast bags on a balloon basket. Often I'm forced to turn into a pub from sheer exhaustion.

"Give me ... just a moment, sorry ... two, four, five, seven, seven-fifty ... hang on ... thirteen ... twenty ... give me three pints. And please, for the love of God, keep the change."

This is not to say that the coins don't come in handy. Payphones (remember those, Yanks?) are great for dropping some euroweight when you have to call ahead to the B&B in Doolin because you took the War of Independence tour and are still in Co. Cork, four pints deep with the tour guide, his wife and children, a French museum curator, an English author and her husband, and the Lord Mayor of Clonakilty.

This may sound like something straight from the Tourist Board, but I assure you it is quite common. My family and I actually did sit down with the proprietors of the Michael Collins Centre and their children, a French museum curator, an English author and her husband, and the Lord Mayor of Clonakilty after a ceremony at the Collins statue in Emmitt Square on a lovely evening, August 22, 2011.

It's a fine fact that in Ireland, you may find yourself bending an elbow with anyone from the local plumber to, well, the Lord Mayor of Clonakilty. Both will have good stories and except for one having grimy nails and the other a sweet silver necklace, you'd be hard pressed to tell the apart. Say hello, stand him a pint (I'd refrain from the coin dump, however, as it tends to upset the ambience), and just relax: you're in for a treat.

You'll probably want to forego the coin dump for this round and just toss the—what is this, a fifty?—on the bar. Soon enough you'll be up for the next round, waving at the pile of bills that have appeared before you and brushing the air at the barkeep in the universal sign for "take this away"—I'm too busy to search for the right bill, just take it out of here—and thoroughly enjoying yourself. You'll get the right change, trust me, and do both you and the barkeep a favor: don't try to tip. He'll wave it away, you'll insist, he'll refuse, you'll insist, and so on. Tipping is an American custom, not an Irish one. If you must do it, leave some coins on the bar when you leave.

Speaking of buying rounds, allow everyone their turn. I learned this on my first trip. In my exuberance to share my joy of finally making it to Ireland I tried to buy every round, throwing my cash around—what is this, a twenty?—like confetti on New Year's Eve. It upsets the social structure. While we visitors may have the best of intentions, it's seen as more ostentatious than generous. Sit down, Yank, we can all afford a round.

This phenomenon usually happens early in the trip, which is a good reason to see Dublin before heading out to the country. You'll have a better chance of not being noticed over the din of the accursed flat screen TV's that are spreading across the island like an electronic plague.

You will also be less noticed if you're on one of the many tours offered in Dubin. I prefer sightseeing at my own pace, but I have taken a tour or two and enjoyed them. Should you wish to partake in one, it's not necessary to have boned up on The 1916 Rising before seeing the GPO or to have read *Ulysses* before joining a Joyce-themed tour. Having tried to read it is good enough, and if someone on the tour claims to have read it all the way through, they're lying. No one has read it, including Joyce.

About that: Joyce was a prankster, I believe. He knew that no one read *Ulysses* but all hailed it as a triumph of literature. "Hmm," thought Joyce, "I bet I can write a book filled with gibberish and still get paid." This is how *Finnegan's Wake* came about. Joyce snickered on his way to the Bank of Ireland until he was run over by the 8:15, 8:25, 8:47, and 9:05 buses to Dalkey that all arrived at 9:37.

Actually, I'm convinced that the language of *Finnegan's Wake* is nothing more than a really t'ick Dublin accent and can be understood only when read aloud. Try it sometime. Just not in the bookstore, or you'll be arrested for public intoxication.

Dublin has many excellent bookstores, which is unsurprising considering the amazing body of literature produced by Irish writers. The area around Trinity College is especially rich with shop after shop offering everything from Druidic culture to Beowulf.

It's fun to watch my fellow visitors in these places. If one can spot an American in an Irish pub on his first day in Ireland, one can spot him in a Dublin bookstore on his second. Not only that, but you can also easily tell which pub crawl he attended last night by his purchases today. An armload of Wilde, Heaney, Behan, and Joyce? Literary tour. A dozen books with "Rising" in the title? He was at the GPO yesterday with on the Rising tour, which I recommend. It starts and ends in the International Bar, which is a cool pub and, really, any tour that features a pub as its terminus is a good tour. Also they serve a great stew, and although they've succumbed to the pox of television, they at least keep the sound off.

One tip about book buying: wait a few days after the tours before you buy—one euro, two, this makes four, sorry, hang on. Let the excitement wear off before purchasing the collected works of Sean O'Casey. "I'll read it on the flight home." No you won't. Just like I've never read the collected works of Oscar Wilde after seeing "A Woman of No Importance" at The Gate. You'll thumb through the pictures on your iPhone and laugh about the things that happened while you were on your way to someplace else, and then you'll fall asleep and dream about sunsets on Galway Bay.

By now you've realized that this section has been only tangentially concerned with the euro. But maybe not. Our unfamiliarity with the euro can be indicative of our unfamiliarity with the Irish, whatever we think we might know from popular culture on our side of the Atlantic. The euro is not much different than the U.S. dollar, much like how the Irish are not much different than Americans.

But there are subtle and important contrasts that we can understand only through experience and exposure to both. And, much like the euro, we can make the incorrect assumption that since we understand Irish-Americans, we therefore understand the Irish.

So take your time with your euros as you should with the Irish. Think about what they are, how they work, and what they represent. Never overlook their value. And don't be fooled by how colorful they are.

Derry, or The Slash, or Together in All But Name

Derry. LondonDerry. Derry/Londonderry. Londonderry/Derry. Tomato, tomahto, potato, potahto. Let's call the whole thing off.

Derry (and I will refer to it as such throughout, which gives you a sense of my political leanings—except it doesn't, which doesn't make much sense, except in the context of the North, where it makes perfect sense) is a fantastic place. It's a county of fabulous beauty, part of the six that make up the nation of Northern Ireland. No, wait. "Nation" is not right. The statelet, maybe. Territory? Possession? Occupied land? Commonwealth? Whatever.

It's also a city with great historical, cultural, and political significance in both the Irish and British psyche. It was in Derry that the citizens held fast against a siege and brought everlasting fame to a few ragamuffin apprentice boys. Derry was the site of Bloody Sunday during The Troubles. Derry is also the home, so the story goes, of the actual Humpty Dumpty. No, not the big talking egg from Lewis Carroll's imagination but rather a huge cannon piece.

The legend has it that the English built a huge cannon atop the stout walls that still surround the city proper and, following the tradition of giving names to impressive weapons, named it Humpty Dumpty. (Humpty Dumpty sat on a wall ….) Some of the folks living outside the walls saw this as something of a threat and got together to try to figure out how to get rid of it. Attacking the city hadn't worked and probably never would as long as those damned apprentices were still around to spoil the surprise.

But the folks on the wrong end of the barrel of that huge gun got the idea to make its size work to their advantage. If we can't blow it up, they reasoned, maybe we can bring it down. And so they went to work on the base of the wall directly under the cannon with their picks and hammers. They would have known quite well how the wall was built, as they were the wretched souls who were forced to build the damned thing in the first place in order to keep themselves out.

Pick pick, hammer hammer, they worked their way into the foundation until the section of wall collapsed and down came the cannon. (Humpty Dumpty had a great fall.) This was quite a shock to the King's citizens, and the city fathers immediately sent their mounted soldiers out to assess the damage and figure out how to fix it. (All the King's soldiers and all the King's men)

Alas, despite their best efforts at moving the huge piece, they finally threw their hands up in frustration, left the gun there, and rebuilt the wall (probably unwittingly using some of the same men who tore it down), minus Humpty. (Couldn't put Humpty together again.)

Is it true? Why not? Events like this were often set to verse in one way or another (see "Ring around the rosy"), and it does make a good bit of sense. I like to think it's true because it fits together so well.

The city of Derry has come a long way since the Catholics under James were laying logs and chains across the River Foyle to keep English supply ships from relieving the besieged citizens inside the walls. From then until the horror of Bloody Sunday in 1972 and too many heartbreaking events that followed has emerged, if not perfect unity, at least a mutual understanding of their differences and an honest and mostly successful attempt to get along today and leave the troubles of yesterday alone. The statue that stands in the middle of town called "Hands Across the Divide" is testament to this. It is symbolic of both sides in the centuries-long conflict between Unionist/Protestant and Nationalist/Catholic reaching out to each other to find peace and understanding and is quite a nice piece. A cynic might point out that the two figures aren't actually shaking hands and never will unless someone creates a new statue, but Derry these days is a vibrant, open, and friendly town with no time for anything but making a quick pound and getting on with the neighbors. I think they ought to move the hands closer a little each day.

Derry is home to some beautiful old churches, remarkably well preserved despite the scarred history surrounding them, and all feature memorials to all those who served and died in battle in World Wars I and II. Another worthwhile site is the Apprentice Boys hall. How I got to explore this fascinating building is a perfect example of the town's pleasant, friendly, and almost shockingly helpful people.

It was on a gorgeous August day in 2001, and my wife and son and I had just finished touring one of the churches. We were stopped on a street corner looking at a tourist map, wondering where to go next, when a nice old gent approached us.

"Hello there," he said in that peculiar sing-song "Nordie" accent. "If you're looking for something to see, head down this street to the Apprentice Boys hall."

He went on to describe what it was, why it was there, and what it held. Marvelous, we said. He continued, "And when you get there, tell them that Paul Johnson sent you and that you want to get on the roof. They don't usually bring the public up there," and at this he grinned and winked, "but let them know that I'll be checking to make sure they did. You can see the entire city and on a rare day like this it's not to be missed!"

We thanked him and said goodbye, by which of course I mean that we chatted for half an hour about where we were from, when did we arrive, how long are we staying, what have we seen, had we had lunch, where to get lunch, where to go after, were we enjoying our stay, where else we'd been, the weather, the best place for souvenirs, had we raingear (might cloud up a bit later), and a dozen other topics that made for yet another unplanned but fabulous experience with yet another but by now unsurprisingly friendly Ulsterman.

We strolled down to the hall. I'd describe it to you, but this is one of those places that should be visited without prior prejudice or expectation. I will say, however, that we were treated like royalty and given a top-to-bottom personal tour. And the view from the roof is spectacular. Paul, I'm sure, was pleased.

Just outside the walls is the neighborhood known as the Bogside. The name itself evokes images of a hardscrabble existence, and although life here has improved considerably since the Troubles, it is still a bit depressing. The Bogside is infamous for the bloody horrors of the Troubles and famous for the many murals that depict the names and faces of the fallen freedom fighters who died in their struggle for civil rights or, depending on one's viewpoint, the names and faces of terrorists and murderers. I will say only that what took place here was a tragedy.

Whether these permanent reminders are a good thing I will leave to the visitor to decide. But their emotional power is undeniable. At the entrance to the area stands the one remaining wall of a housing estate long since torn down. Black letters on the whitewashed wall inform the visitor that "You Are Now Entering Free Derry."

Fear not. Though the area can be charitably described as working class, it is quite safe and the residents are as nice down here as they are up inside the town walls.

We strolled along the streets, pausing at each mural and the various memorials and meeting people. Though initially more reticent than the average Irish, once engaged they are as loquacious and friendly as any, eager to describe the sights, where to go next, how old is the little feller, and are you after having your supper because the chipper down the road is excellent.

I decided to visit to Bogside Inn, the unofficial headquarters of the area. My son decided that he'd rather climb the hundreds of steps up to the wall. My wife volunteered to go with him. She climbed the steps but declined to join in him rolling back down the hill. She told me later he did it nine times. And it's a good-sized hill. He snored all the way back to Letterkenny. Two points for my wife.

Anyway, I entered the inn. It was dark after the sunshine. I was disappointed to see those damned televisions over the bar, but realized that I should have expected that by now and besides, what did I expect to see—five guys in black masks sticking timers on a car bomb? I adjusted my attitude and took a stool.

The place was mostly empty, just two gents at the bar and another couple of guys at a table. The barkeep looked up from his paper, nodded at me, and went back to reading. I'd been in-country for a while so I took this in stride. He'd get to me when he finished the article. And he did.

"Howerya?"

"Fine, thanks. I'll have a Budweiser, please." Please forgive me, but I was tired of stout.

I have to assume it was my accent and not my desire for an American beer but all four sets of eyes were suddenly on me.

"American, is it?" said the gent to my right. It is, I said.

"First time?" For the first time, I hesitated before answering a question. It was my first time in Derry, but not my first time in, where? Ireland? UK? Northern Ireland? Ulster? I decided on honest ignorance.

"It's my first time in Derry but not in … how do I put it?" I shrugged and raised my eyebrows. "Ireland? The North? I don't want to insult anyone."

The old gent down the bar to my left answered for me. "It's all right, 'Ireland' is fine." He raised his glass. "We're all Irishmen in here, anyway."

Then he asked me the question I was really hoping to avoid. "So what's your name?"

Oy. I smiled ruefully. "Gerry Britt," I said.

"Ah, Jaysus!" yelled the bartender as he slapped his paper down, which made everyone, including me, laugh. "One 't' or two?" More laughter.

I held up two fingers and smiled. "Two."

The guy on my right gave me an exaggerated squint. "You look like an Irishman. And where are your people from?"

Thank God for easy questions. "County Tipp," I said. "And they got thrown off their land like everyone else down there."

"Well, that's good, then," said the guy down the end to more laughter and then, to the barkeep, "Give him his pint, he can stay!" Laughs again. This was going well.

My friend on the right slid down next to me, smiled a big toothy grin, and put his hand on my shoulder. "We're just takin' the piss, Yank. Those times are past. The bad days."

"Well that's good because I'm on vacation and getting my ass kicked is not on my list of things to do."

A good joke at one's own expense goes a long way in Ireland, north or south. The comment was well received. I raised my glass. "Thank you for the warm welcome!"

"To the bad days," said the old gent, raising his own glass.

One of the men at the table raised his glass. "The good old bad days!"

We settled into easy conversation. Where are you from in the States, when did you get here … well, you know it by now. Soon all four of us were huddled at the table and I was treated to a grand old time. The chat was glorious. I chimed in here and there when a question or comment was directed to me, but mostly I listened. The conversation was entertaining, lively, and utterly fascinating. They talked about life in the Bogside before, during, and after the Troubles. I was mesmerized by the old gent as he told tales that went back to the 1930s. Truly amazing stuff.

When I glanced at my watch, I was shocked to realize I'd been there two hours. It seemed like only minutes, but it was time to go. I made my farewells. It took another twenty minutes to get out the door and I had to promise to visit the Bogside artists' studio before they'd let me go. The visit to the Inn remains one of my warmest memories.

When I stepped outside I was surprised by the daylight, but it was only late afternoon. I walked over to my wife who was sitting on the bottom of the steps.

"Where's the boy?" I asked.

She pointed up the hill. "He'll be here in a minute."

I followed her finger and there he was, my own little Humpty Dumpty, having a great fall.

I told her I had to visit the artists' studio. That was another very interesting time, but I'll give you only one memorable bit. As I sat and chatted with one of the men who actually painted the murals, he lit a cigarette. Because smoking indoors is barred in the North like it is in the Republic, I commented on it. "I thought you weren't allowed to smoke indoors?"

He waved a dismissive hand. "This is Free Derry."

Ah, the People...

The Irish can be described in many ways. Stereotypes will tell us they are stubborn but easygoing, open but secretive, and fun-loving but moody. In other words, just as contradictory and human as anyone else. There are, however, some characteristics and habits that are exclusively Irish.

Pay attention to speech habits. There are some peculiarly Irish ways of speaking, such as adding, "what?" to the end of a sentence. This is not a sign of deafness but rather a shortened way of saying, "Do you understand what I mean?" Similarly, where Americans have inserted "like" into every sentence and become Valley Girl Nation, the Irish will more often add the "like" at the end of the phrase, so that the American "My eyes are like, so puffy after last night's hooley," becomes "My eyes are all puffy, like, from last night's hooley."

Another interesting thing is the way the Irish ask about the length of your stay. Where an American would ask, "How long are you staying?" the Irish will want to know "When are you leaving?" Don't be put off—no one's counting the days until you're gone.

Other Irish-English words most likely to give Yanks pause are "howerya?" and "after." The former is simply

"How are you?" all squished together. It requires no lengthy response about your physical or mental condition at that moment. In fact, they really don't care any more than you do when you ask the bank teller back home how they are. The latter is used to describe their present condition based on a prior activity such as "I'm after having my dinner." I've already eaten, thanks.

Irish roads are an interesting proposition. Although the EU cash that flooded into the country during the boom helped improve the national road system (steamrolling some important historical sites in the process), there are at least three categories of road that range from not bad to god-awful. The "M"-designated motorways are comparable to U.S. highways in quality and safety, and the "N" roads are mostly equivalent to U.S. local roads. Mostly. Although there are many places where the nice, two-full-lane, lined road is fast and efficient, there are also many places where the "N" road winds and twists and narrows and makes you wonder if you didn't somehow miss a turn back in Cashel.

The rural side roads that branch off the better roads are fun and exciting. Sometimes an "R"-designated road will have almost two full lanes, albeit bordered by tall hedges that are sometimes too dense to walk through and more often impossible to walk through because there's a stone wall behind them. There are two classes of rural road: small and big. The big road has a white line down the middle. The small road has a strip of grass down the middle. There is an inverse relationship between the height of the grass strip and the width of the road. It's fun to watch the grass get higher as the lane narrows into a one lane, as if perspective has gone on vacation and you're disappearing into a painting. Ah, yes, here I am in rural Ireland, traveling down a country lane in a bucolic setting that—GAAAAAAA!—

Here you might come across that other feature of Irish roads: the Killer Tractor, appearing from nowhere and hurtling at you over a rise at incredible speed, front wheels scratching and clawing and sliding along the gravel and perpetually wet grass, with hay bales stacked impossibly high and swaying to and fro, driven by a kid who appears to be 12 years old. Luckily, there's no time to panic or even react beyond folding in your elbows to get as skinny as possible while pointing the car into a space between tractor and hedge that no car, no motorcycle, could ever possibly fit and—ohthankyougod—you're through and ready to enjoy the countryside again, as soon as your heart rate gets below 150 bpm and the quart of adrenaline coursing through your veins drains out and your cheeks unclench. No, the other ones. Encounter enough tractors and you'll also notice that they only do Warp 5 when they're full. On the way back, empty, they putter along and will even edge over to give you more room to get around from the opposite direction. Do not expect this courtesy when one is in front of you, however. The driver, having dropped off his load, has nothing more on his mind than a cold pint and does not notice, or care, that he's meandering all over the road, effectively cutting off any chance of you passing him. Just relax, shove it into second gear, and try to stay far enough back to avoid the spray of moldy hay floating in front of you.

The only thing in the rural areas that travels faster than a full tractor is news. The 'hedge telegraph is verbal broadband, especially if you're from out of town. By the time you get back to the B&B after a night of singing every John Denver song you know ("Take Me Home, Country Roads" is always a big hit) and downing one too many stouts, the entire village will know about it. They'll ask you what you did last night but, trust me, they already know and are asking only to see if your version corresponds to the version they heard. Don't bother with details, as you'll hear them soon enough and you might as well get the official version, which is sometimes close to the truth but is rarely gathered from anything you might contribute.

Keep word of mouth in mind when renting a car at the airport. An inconspicuous vehicle is good. A neon-green, box-shaped minivan is bad. I made this mistake once and was told where I was at every minute of every day because my vehicle stuck out like a sore thumb. I thought about swapping cars with a local for a night, just to throw them off, but even that would have been discovered before the first scones were ready at the village shop.

Another bit to remember is that in the Irish countryside, everyone knows everyone else. So the lady in GAA shop in Tipperary town knows the owner of the pub where you slaughtered "Take Me Home, Country Roads." This may explain the modesty of the Irish: you can't puff up your achievements or downplay your antics when the stranger you're speaking to knows more about it than you do.

When speaking to someone, don't make the mistake of thinking that a seemingly innocent or naïve-sounding question is a demonstration of Irish simplicity. They do this partly for your benefit and partly to take the piss out of you. I was once in a pub in Kilcommon, drinking with an old friend with both of his original eyes and a new friend with one. This matters by the way, but give us a moment. An obvious American walked in asking for directions to the Limerick road. Emmet, my one-eyed friend, asked him if he was driving or walking. Driving, said the American. Ah, well, that's the best way, replied Emmett. The furrowed brow of my countryman made Emmitt smile and me laugh. A legitimate but ridiculous question designed to both help and hinder. Classic Irish.

Later, Emmett showed me his unoriginal eye. Literally. Had it in the palm of his hand. I have the picture, and no, it's not included here. Eye in or eye out, Emmett is common in that a friendly jab or poke in your conversational eye is part of the language. Be warned: bragging will not be tolerated nor ignored, so boast about your career and huge house at your own peril.

A fine way of avoiding such talk is to keep your alcohol intake at your usual level. Too many people who visit Ireland do so with an ugly stereotype stamped in their head: that of the Irishman as boozehound. This stems from the caricatures of the nineteenth century perpetuated by the likes of the *Saturday Evening Post* and other Anglo-Saxon publications, designed to portray the immigrant Irish as clowns and buffoons who want nothing more than a crappy job and a good drunk down at the pub. True, many Irish did drink too much in America in those days, but it was mostly from struggling in a strange city, alone, and far from a family and home that they'll never see again. You'd drink, too.

But aside from selling alcohol, the Irish-American pub has little in common with the Irish pub. The pub in Ireland serves as much more than a place that offers alcohol. It is meeting place, catering hall, funeral home, voting booth, debate club, and poker room. Engagements are celebrated, 5-year energy plans are formed, toasts are made to the recently departed, and the most complicated card games in the world are played (see below). Most go to the pub to talk, visit, and catch up on the latest news. Drinks are sipped, not downed. It is not necessary to pound pints in order to fit in, and you'll look a bit foolish by doing so.

I've mentioned some pub etiquette points elsewhere, but allow me to go into greater detail here and offer a few particular suggestions, some learned the hard way. I'll preface these by saying that they are true almost everywhere except for the more touristy pubs in the cities, where the clientele is apt to be less local. The first and most important thing is to relax. Don't stand at the bar waving your money around, trying to get the barkeep's attention. Trust me, he (or she) sees you and will get to you soon enough. If you're in that much of a hurry you're in the wrong place anyway. Have a seat. Take in your surroundings. The photos on the wall, the ancient relics that hang everywhere, and the good people around you. A nod will suffice as a greeting. You may feel a bit uncomfortable the first time, as if every eye is upon you. They are. You're a bit of a novelty, after all, and you were most likely tagged as visitor the second you walked in. But there's no need to feel discomfited. Sometimes the best way to start a conversation is to say nothing at all. Americans can be a bit too friendly, too quickly, for Irish tastes. You're an outsider, and if you accept that and don't try to immediately ingratiate yourself, you'll be appreciated for it. Sit quietly while your Guinness settles and you can bet that someone will say hello or ask you if you're "on holiday" before your pint is set before you. The greeting or question will come with a smile, and the smile and the interest are genuine.

The Irish really are a friendly, hospitable people. The best description of this was given to me by a barman from Upperchurch. I'd been in the village a few days by then and the barman, Richie, inquired as to my impressions of the place so far. "It's beautiful here," I had said, "but what's impressed me the most are the people. Everyone—and I mean everyone—has been nothing but friendly and hospitable to me from the moment I arrived. You don't see that everywhere in the world. Most places, you have to prove yourself a bit before folks will let you into their circle."

"Ah, they're good people here," Richie agreed. Then he said something that perfectly sums up the Irish. "Around here, we give you goodwill on credit. After that, it's up to you to earn it."

Ireland is famous for its saints and scholars, but no poet ever said it better.

Soon enough you'll find yourself in pleasant conversation with the barman, the gent to your right, the couple sitting behind you, and the two guys that just sat down next to you. It's not necessary to give them your entire life story at once. Allow it to come gently, slowly.

This is the true beauty of Ireland: a pace that lets the soul relax. Sip it in, like you're doing with that pint of black nectar in front of you.

Soon enough your glass will be empty, or close enough to empty that you'll motion for another. You may offer to buy a round for your new friends, but it's quite possible that your offer will be waved off and someone will stand you the next pint. Accept it graciously. The next round can be yours. The one after that should not be. Pub etiquette demands that each of the group buys a round in turn. Do not upset this by insisting on showing your appreciation of their company by throwing your board game money around. If you want to share, buy a bag or two of crisps—potato chips—and spread open both bags on the bar for all to share. The same works for chips—french fries to you and me.

Along the lines of words and phrases, eventually you'll need to empty your insides. You'll want to ask for the toilet, not the bathroom, which is where one in Ireland would, as the name implies, take a bath. Your companions may wander off to the toilet for a moment or disappear for five or ten minutes into the smoking area.

Technically, smoking areas are supposed to be outdoor areas but, like so many words in Ireland, "outdoors" is open to interpretation. Most pubs may have started with outdoor smoking areas that were open to the elements, but these days they more often define it to mean that rain could, if it tried really hard, drip into the room. At some point. Eventually. Now the smoking areas have become nothing more than extensions of the pub a few yards away from the main room, comfortably decked out, often with fireplaces, snugs, and jukeboxes, with many-layered cantilevered half-roofs to keep out all but the most insistent precipitation.

Whether you smoke or not, join them in the smoking room now and then. Many patrons will spend the entire evening in there. The first time I walked into one I thought I wandered into a marijuana den. Everyone was either smoking or rolling their own, and it took me a minute to realize that they were only avoiding the high prices of packaged cigarettes by smoking pouch tobacco. If you do smoke, trade a Marlboro for a hand-rolled Virginia Gold. If you're really brave and don't mind having the piss taken out of you, try rolling one yourself. Good luck, especially with getting the itsy-bitsy filter to stay in the tip.

The gentle ribbing that the Irish enjoy giving to visitors is harmless and often a sign that they're enjoying your company. You'll hear more words and phrases that you won't understand, but the phrasing is often beautiful so enjoy the melody if not the meaning. And don't worry too much if you don't understand every word that is said. Irish accents can be much harder to decipher than what you hear in the movies. Notice the plural, accents. There is no such thing as a single Irish accent. There is a Dublin accent (actually there are a few Dublin accents), which is not too hard for an American to recognize and understand. The Midlands accent can be a bit more difficult, and even the locals will have trouble with some of the more rural farmers. The Cork accent, on the other hand, is a completely different language. Don't feel too bad about asking, "Sorry?" and tilting your ear towards the speaker. He's used to it and won't mind a bit, as nothing pleases a Corkman more than the sound of his own voice. Just ask a Kerryman. The only accent you should use is your own. The Irish lilt that you amaze your friends with around St. Patrick's Day sounds to the Irish like an American tourist trying to imitate an English actor trying to imitate an Irishman.

The people are Ireland's greatest natural resource. When exported they build nations. At home they are genuine, hospitable, and helpful. Spend time getting to know them and the Ireland will soon envelop and relax you. And then, if you're really lucky, you can try your hand at…

Irish Poker

Start with four dairy farmers, two publicans, one heavy equipment dealer, a councilor, and a garage owner. Sprinkle in a retired beer distributor, one used car salesman, and a grocery shop owner. Add one overwhelmed American. Mix well. After removing the black 6s, 8s, and Js, blend the remaining cards into two other full decks. Be sure that the cards are at least 10 years old. Shuffle them haphazardly. Deal. Oh, by the way: deuces, treys, and the 6, 7, 8, 9, and 10 of diamonds are wild. Jacks or better. You're the buy-in, Yank. How many cards will you have?

Oh. Okay. I'll take ... wait. What?

Welcome to Irish poker night.

Except for kitchen table trad sessions, poker night is my favorite kind of gathering. My adopted pub-away-from-home holds them weekly. Billed as a tournament, it starts at 10:00 p.m., and it's in the Irish countryside. The last description makes the other two slightly misleading, of course. There *is* a tournament, but that's really just a part of the evening. And it certainly won't start at 10:00 p.m.

I was invited to my first night once the pub owners were assured of two things: first, that I was not likely to blab about it to the local authorities, and second, that I was not likely to win. I was assured that "It's just a friendly game with some of the locals, nothing big."

Yeah, right.

I smiled and accepted the offer for the following night, doing my best to act like I actually believed her. I didn't find it necessary to burden her with the fact that I've played cards my entire life and knew two things for certain: there is no such thing as a friendly card game, and although a tournament is a nice reason to get together, it's the games before and after that really gather the crowd. Especially when there's going to be fresh American pigeon being served on a platter, stuffed with money.

"What's the buy-in?" I asked.

"50 Euro." Quite reasonable. Friendly, even. I waited.

"Sometimes there'll be a small game before or after." Oh, really? I waited.

"Y'know, they'll play for a bit of cash before everyone gets here."

A bit of cash. Got it. "Should I bring a bit of cash with me, then?"

"Oh, if you want, but you don't need to. Only if you'd like to sit in for a few hands." Uh huh.

I arrived at the pub around 9:30 the next evening. It was crowded for a weeknight. Looking around, I saw that it was mostly older couples except for a half-dozen women gathered around a table in the corner, glasses of sherry in hand and a soft candle flickering between them. I wondered where their spouses were. I peeked into the back room. Six gents sat around an identical table, but instead of glasses of sherry they had cards in hand and a nice pile of euros between them. I couldn't see every bill, but what I could see put the pot well over 200 euro. They were playing five-card draw. I watched the last two players get two apiece. 200 euro in the middle before the draw. *"Sometimes there'll be a small game before or after."* Okay.

I watched the hand play out. Everybody was in and it got checked around to the last player. He was a big man in a red V-neck sweater and he smiled as he bet 60 euro, revealing a great set of pearly white choppers. Fold, fold, fold, fold, fold. Choppers bought the pot. Six players in and not one made their hand? I thought about going back to the cottage for more cash.

I made some hellos and howeryas and when are ya leavings and sipped a tea with milk. Jimmy the owner came out to say hello and we chatted about the game. "Are you playing tonight?" he said.

"I am," I replied. Back in America, I would have said "yes." In all my trips over, this particular way of responding was the speech habit that I fell into most quickly and tended to keep longer after I left. Did you fix that light? I did. Said in Ireland, it simply conveys yes or no. Said in America, it indicates irritation. There are a few other words and phrases that have become part of my everyday speech, but I use most of those not out of habit but because I love the way they sound. Mad for a slash. Mind yourself, now. How's she cuttin'? Sound. Ah, no bother.

Jimmy leaned in and gave me a one-eyed squint and the hint of a smile. "Don't hurt 'em too bad, now, Gerry," and he winked. "We'll need 'em back after you're gone."

I smiled and winked back. "Just enough to pay for the trip."

Jimmy laughed, then said with the squint—but no trace of the smile—"You know your way around a card table, I'm guessing."

"I've been known to play a hand or two." I winked and let a grin come through. "But no one here needs to know that now, do they?"

He slapped me on the back. "I'm staying away from you!" he said, and nodded towards the door. "You'll have your name on the sign. It'll be on the sign and I'll be behind the bar." He was enjoying himself now, like he sometimes did when he invented scenarios—"I'll be behind bar running my legs off"—now he was rolling, one hand squeezing my shoulder, the other fist bumping my chest—"dreaming of the day when my debt to the Yank"—now he put in face in his hands—"when my debt to that Yank is finally paid off! Ohhhhh!" And he laughed and slapped my back as Siobhan, his wife (who blames me for her bad behavior, but that's another tale), wandered past.

"Jeezus, Yank, what are doing to my poor husband?"

"Taking his pub."

She raised her eyes to the ceiling. "From your lips to God's ears. We'd be shut of this place and I'd live longer."

"Oh, you wouldn't know what to do with yourself," Jimmy said.

"I'd get away from *this* Yank, that's sure."

Jimmy affected a soothing voice. "Ah, now. Don't be picking on the man." He put his arm around me. "He's a guest in our country and—"

She cut across him, "Guest, my arse. He's been causing me grief since he got here—how many times is it now, Gerry, you've been here?"

"Let's see." I counted on my fingers. "Five."

Jimmy put his other arm around me. "Y'see that? You know what that is? That's loyalty to home" (I got a nice squeeze) "and to family" (another squeeze).

"Loyal load of shite is what that is," Siobhan muttered, but she was trying not to smile and Jimmy caught it.

He squeezed and shook me. "Loyalty!"

"To home and family," I agreed.

Siobhan shook her head in mock frustration. "Why don't ya's both go home and leave me "—then sotto voce—"*the feck alone.*" And we all laughed like idiots.

While we were amusing ourselves, three more gents had joined the table. Nine players and what looked like more than one deck. What the hell?

Jimmy gave me one last slap on the back. "I've got to go, Gerry. I've a few things to get sorted in the back. I'll see ya later." He pointed at the card game. "Don't hurt 'em, now." Then he winked and disappeared just like

Santa Claus, except in a wrinkled white shirt and shapeless trousers.

I sipped the last of my tea and tried to figure out the game. It was still five-card draw. With 9 players eligible for 8 cards each, they needed 72 cards. With the decrepit cards, I couldn't tell from the thickness if there was a deck and a half or two full decks.

I sidled up and listened to the chatter. I've developed a decent ear for most accents on the island (certain places in west Cork excepted), but trying to follow these guys was impossible. Money flew into and out of the pot. The dealer gave the deck a perfunctory hand-to-hand shuffle, slapped it on the table, and said something I didn't catch to the man on his right, who tapped the deck and replied indecipherably. The cards were dealt in a small circle, nine hands counted out (this I understood)—onetotreeferfiseeksivayenine—and pushed to each player. A frantic repositioning of cards followed as all arranged their hand.

The betting went around at light speed:

Dealer, to the player on his immediate left: "Martin!"

Martin: "No."

And the next seven:

"No."

"No."

"No."

"No."

"No."

"Yes. Twenty."

"No." Cards folded.

And once more around:

"No." Fold.

"Just a small one, thanks, Jimmy. No no, I've still got a bit—"

"Martin!"

"What? Oh. No." Fold.

"No." Fold.

"No." Fold.

"Yes." Two tens float into the middle.

"No." Fold.

"How many, Phil?"

"One."

"Michael?"

"Three, please."

"Michael."

"Forty."

"Phil?"

"No." Fold.

Michael showed an ace, a two, a ten, and two sixes, threw his cards down, and scooped up what might have been a correct pot to the general approval (far as I could tell) of the other players. The entire hand took maybe 30 seconds. The next hand was started before my brain was able to process what had just happened.

I tapped a player on the shoulder and nodded towards Michael. "What did he have?"

"Three sixes." Three?

"Something wild?"

"Yes, twos." Okay, that made sense.

"And the three, four, five, and six of diamonds." Oh, okay. Wait. What?

My confusion must have been obvious, and he smiled and gestured to an open spot on the banquette. "You'll learn it quicker if you play. Are you here for the tournament?"

My reply was interrupted by Tommy, the car salesman, with whom I was friendly. "Padraig, do you not know Gerry? From America? He's one of the Britts from down Drombane." Tommy waved vaguely south.

"Tommy!"

"What?" Apparently the next hand was rolling through.

Tommy looked down, surprised to see five cards in his hands. Where did these come from? He seemed unperturbed. A quick glance. "No." Fold. "You know the Britts." Padraig looked doubtful. "You do know them," Tommy insisted. Padraig still looked doubtful. "You do! Janie Britt, down Holycross way," he gestured vaguely west.

"I don't," insisted Padraig the still doubtful. Now Tommy was perturbed.

"You do! Janie Britt—down in the home—in Holycross—"

"Yeah, I know the home in Holycross. Do you think I'm stupid?"

"One thing at a time, now," replied Tommy, which got a laugh from everyone at the table, none of whom had given any indication that they were aware of our conversation or, in fact, anything beyond the game. Tommy persisted. "Janie Britt, lived in Drombane." He gestured vaguely south again. "You follow that, now."

"I do, yes," replied Padraig.

"Well, that's a good start." More laughter. Someone won a hand with five 9s. Sheesh. "When her husband died—John Britt—" Tommy looked at Padraig inquiringly.

Padraig nodded. "Two years ago, wasn't it?" He elbowed the man next to him, a stout guy in an ancient white button-down. Euros were crammed in the breast pocket. "Remember that one, Phil? At the hall?"

"I don't," said Phil, organizing his cards. If all the wild cards were still in play, he had five aces, none of them an actual ace. Maybe I should have brought more money.

"You do, you were there!" The question of Padraig's knowledge of my relatives was now forgotten as the subject turned to what was apparently a hell of a wake for the late John Britt. Tommy tapped me on the arm and quietly said, "Gerry, sit. Play a few hands. I'll get Padraig sorted later. He's a bit thick."

"I'm not!"

"You are. Thick!" *T'ick*. And so it went.

I squeezed in next to Tommy, who introduced me to everyone. Phil, Seamus, Padraig, Martin, Sneezy, Doc. I shook hands with those I could reach, nodded to the others. "I hope there's not a test later," I commented.

"If they take your money, you'll remember them," Martin—or maybe it was Pat—said.

"Then I hope I forget everybody."

Martin (or Pat) dealt the cards as I laid my cash on the table.

We played for an hour and I thoroughly enjoyed myself. I tried to follow the game while I engaged in the conversation around the table and failed miserably at both, so I concentrated on my cards first, joining or rejoining the chatter between hands or whenever I folded, which was often. Tommy continued to pester Padraig until he, Tommy, was satisfied that Padraig understood which Britts were under discussion. This took a good while, but I suspect Padraig was being deliberately t'ick. I think Tommy was suspicious, too. "Stop it now. You're not as thick as that."

"Yes he is," said Phil.

I was peppered with questions about my family and regaled with tales of possible, probable, and definite cousins once, twice, thrice removed. I discovered that I was related to almost everyone at the table through blood or marriage. I felt myself settling deeper into this wonderful world and it thrilled me.

Mind Yourself, Now

I've been fortunate to spend a lot of time in Ireland. While so much has become familiar, there is still so much to experience. Each time I'm there each of my senses experience something new and I never fail to learn something important (well, eventually). Some of these experiences and lessons were planned, but—and if I've made any impression with my scribblings here, I hope it's this one—most were not. This is not to say that you should skip the Cliffs of Moher or Temple Bar. You should not. But Ireland is a place where the in-between is something special. I will, if asked, lovingly describe the intense colors of the Books of Kells, the hush of the viewing room, and the sense of awe and respect (reverence?) that overcomes seventy-five year old scholars and eighteen year old backpackers. But the Book of Kells won't pop into my mind when I hear "My Little Honda 50" or taste parsnips. I'll think of the songs around Brian's kitchen table at 4am. I'll remember eating dinner in front of a coal fire with himself and Batty, watching Stargate on the telly while outside the rain came sideways out of the dark. Or John dancing on a chair, banging on the bodhran like it needed to be banged on, miming every verse of "Wild Colonial Boy" while six of us tortured the lyrics. One memory will lead to another. 5am, the pub door long since bolted, but inside sat a good dozen of us doing our best to harmonize "Blue Bayou." Did a fine job of it, too. You didn't. We did!

There's so many…will you stay for one more pint? You will? "Lovely," as Noel O'Brien, the best banjo player (and taxi driver, group rates available, 24-hour on call) in Munster is fond of saying, often from inside an empty tub while the other 75% of the soon-to-be-famous trad group "Four ****s In a Toilet" perfect their debut CD. Well, now, here's to Maria for yelling from the kitchen to her man at the front door when I dropped in 'anytime.' "Jesus, it's the Yank! Would you tell him that when we say 'drop in any time, we don't really *mean* it!"

Just the introductions to new people can be entertaining. One evening at Kennedy's in Upperchurch , "Gerry, I'd like you meet Phil Ryan—he's in charge of the walking tours; Margaret Sweeney—she writes our community blogs; and Conn Ryan, a relation to Phil here. Oh, is he not, Margaret? Sorry, Phil. Anyway, Conn's a retired private detective. So left to right, you have Phil the Walker, Maggie the Talker, and Conn the Stalker."

Little snippets of conversation are also the gates to a reservoir of memories. A sweet, tiny, elderly lady ran the gift shop at Holycross. She gave us directions to Bohernacrusha. "Head down the big road," and here she leaned forward and slowly moved a hand forward, "--and you'll know it's the big road because there's a white line down the middle," Good to know. More on that in a moment, but back to our guide, "and you'll come to a crossroads. There will be a pub on each side. Go between the pubs," here came the hand again and she said it again for emphasis, "go betweeeeeen the pubs—don't stop at them, now!" The hand now wagged a finger at me. "But go between the pubs and Anna's place will be on the left."

Excellent! Wait. "Anna's?"

"The Stakelum place. The B&B. That's where you'll be staying?"

"Yes, but how did you know—"

"Why else would you be going to Bohernacrusha? It's only got her place and the two pubs. And you don't want to be stopping at *them*." We went betweeeeeen the pubs—we didn't stop--and got there safely. We stopped at the pubs later, though.

A few words about the big road. The line down the middle of the road, or the absence of one, will tell you more about that road than any Michelin map. First, there are wide, safe, state highway-type roads with double lines. The Irish drive very fast on these roads. A single line tells you that there are mostly, usually, two full lanes, and you're probably safe from most oncoming tractor traffic. The Irish drive very fast on these roads, too.

If there is no line, you're only guaranteed a lane and sometimes most of a second. Here the Irish drive even faster because there's not much traffic and you can still take the turns on four wheels. The Tractor Factor is high on these roads, and for the same reasons. Unless you're very familiar with these roads, pull over for anyone coming the other way and also anyone coming up behind you, because they want to get the hell home from work and you, ya feckin' rental car drivin' eejit, are delaying them.

And the most the important rule of the road: If you find yourself on a road with a grass strip, just stay on it. This is the in-between time. You're on an adventure and you never know what might happen.

So take care, be patient, and you'll enjoy an Ireland that many don't take the time to see.

Mind yourself, now.

Avoiding the PITS*: A Handy Guide to Beating the Blues after the Green (*Post-Ireland Travel Syndrome)

You've just returned from your dream holiday in Ireland. The flight was long, you've wrestled the luggage into the house (including the one purchased on the last day to hold all the sweaters), tossed your carry-on with the jacket you wore to the airport on the kitchen chair, and flopped down in the living room, contemplating unpacking. "What a trip!" you think, followed closely by "Man, that's a lot of luggage," and ending with "I need a [insert favorite beverage]."

This is the crucial moment of your trip. And it is definitely part of your trip. For this point is when you may succumb to a common holiday pitfall: the post-vacation blues. It's a rotten feeling after any vacation. But it's especially sharp when the blues come after all the greens of Ireland. Not to mention the whites of the smiles, the reds of the trim on the pub windows, and the yellow of the Co. Clare hurlers' jerseys. Fear not: here's my handy guide to surviving this stage.

Tip #1: Just the phrase "Tip #1" is enough to make anyone smile, because it's so true (think about it…). But here it is: unpack slowly. It's a practical tip to keep from breaking the Kerry turf Christmas ornament, Waterford crystal, Belleek china, four-pack of Guinness pint glasses, Wicklow seashells, and Giant's Causeway snowglobe. But it's also a nice recap of your journey. Unfold all the new T-shirts, hoodies, sweaters, caps, scarves, and jackets. That little shop in Kilkenny comes to mind, the one with the old gent who told you where to find the best trad session that night, where you learned the bodhran without embarrassment and drank in the craic along with the dark foamy stuff. The place in Kenmare springs up, with the lady who told you firmly that no, no—green is not your color, get the blue, and not that one, the one your wife looked at.

Look at the postcards in the Avoca bag—Irish shops have great bags, don't they?—that you forgot to send. Remember Killarney National Park (breathtaking!), Slea Head (and you thought nothing could top Killarney), Newgrange (I hope I win the solstice drawing), and Grafton Street (the Tart with the Cart! Love that Dublin humor).

Tip #2: Gather all your paperwork from the trip. Nothing works better as a travelogue. Look at your passport stamp and remember the feeling when you first landed: I'm here! I'm finally here. Gaze at the car rental receipt: your first real encounter with a real, live Irish person…and a real, live Irish accent, when you're first words were "Good morning, I have a reservation" and your next were "I'm sorry, what?" Or possibly your first real encounter with an Eastern European–Dublin accent, in which case you just nodded politely, signed where you were told, and read all the papers in the shuttle van. In either case, it will bring a smile.

Unfold the map and pat yourself on the back. You really did okay with whole sit-on-the-right, drive-on-the-left thing, after all. Sure, the first few roundabouts were an adventure—especially taking the third exit (what do the parentheses mean, again? Is this the N21?)—and you forgot to pay the M50 toll for two days, costing you an extra few Euro, but you remembered to move over for the natives and keep to the left on the highway—er, motorway (let's see…sixth-tenths of a mile per kilometer, carry the decimal). And the parking discs were fascinating—we should have those here! Here's the business card from the B&B, where the phrase "You can settle up in the morning" introduced you to Irish ways, you enjoyed figuring out how to work the shower, and the conversation with the German couple at breakfast was fascinating. Receipts from Christchurch (was that really Strongbow?) and the Viking bus (I can't believe I wore that helmet), the Rock of Cashel tour and the cheese from the artisan market in Cork, and the Giant's Causeway and Belfast buses. Hey, here's a bookmark from that place in Sligo, now where's the book? Here it is! Some Yeats before bed is perfect.

Tip #3: Put the pictures on the laptop. No, do it now. Pile up all your dirty laundry while they load. Then click away while enjoying another glass of [insert favorite beverage here]. Doing this helps imprint the little things that happened in the midst of the big things. The pub after the Cliffs of Moher and the wits in the smoking area. Hey, here's those crazy kids jumping into the Liffey. Oh my God, look at Inishmore, where you got that green sweater while your wife wasn't looking. Notice the difference in your posture and smile as you fell into the Irish rhythm.

By day 2, you understood that Irish friendliness and hospitality were not Board Failte promotions. They were realities. By day 3, you knew that "the tour starts promptly at 4:00" really meant "the tour will start when the guide gets back, he'll be just a moment" and you just smiled and chatted with the family from Oregon in a voice that had lost its American volume and urgency.

Look at all the pictures with your entire party in them, captured by trading cameras with travelers from all over the world. Sometimes it was done by pantomime, offering your camera and gesturing to theirs. But the smiles of understanding and happy agreement made it easy. They're not any different after all. The vistas of Ireland are stunning in any language. Thank you! Danke! Oh, Stockholm, I'd love to go there! Cheers! Yes, first time here, isn't it beautiful? Where are you headed next? Doolin? It's famous for the music, stop at O'Connor's.

Tip #4: Page through the travel book. Unless you booked a coach tour, you'll have a good laugh looking at your planned itinerary, especially your travel time. Smile, and remember next time to include the following in your driving calculations:

a. Sheep that stop in the middle of the road and just…look at you.

b. Stops in every picturesque little town and hamlet.

c. Twenty-minute roadside conversations with locals about directions (and the weather, hydrangeas, the state of the country, where you're headed and why, where you're coming from and why, how you're enjoying your holiday, and their sister who's been to Illinois), all of them blithely unconcerned about the tractors hurtling by with swaying loads of hay piled impossibly high.

Sure, it was a shame that you couldn't get to the Jameson distillery, but it couldn't have topped watching the argument at the pub about the comparative merits of horse breeding in Kildare versus Tipperary. And you got your taste of Jameson's anyway when you got drawn into the talk and came in on the Kildare side: "Aha! Y'see,

Declan! Even the Americans agree with me! Give the Yank here a drink; he's obviously a man of great taste and refinement! Slainte!" Besides, after you realize what you just couldn't get to, you'll have the greatest realization of all (see Tip #5).

Tip #5: You have to go back!

About the Author

Gerry Britt was made in America from Irish parts. His frequent travels to Ireland have been featured on numerous Irish travel and tourist sites. He recently realized a dream by obtaining his Irish citizenship. A native of New York City, he resides in Virginia with his wife, son, and dog, amid photos of Michael Collins, too many Aran sweaters, and rocks pilfered from his grandparents' cottages in Tipperary and Kilkenny.

Made in the USA
Lexington, KY
13 February 2015